Conquest
over
Hatred

Conquest over Hatred

The Donnie Williams Story

Tom Bleecker
Foreword by Joe Hyams

Gilderoy Publications
Capistrano Beach, California

Gilderoy Publications
P. O. Box 7164
Capistrano Beach, California 92624

15 14 13 12 11 10 09 08 07 06   5 4 3 2 1

Library of Congress Control Number: 2006933190

ISBN-13: 978-0-9653132-5-4
ISBN-10: 0-9653132-5-5

First edition published 2006

Designed by Ketsy Sitanggan
www.ketsydesign.com

To my mother Lissie who, beginning in my early childhood, taught me about God. To my mother-in-law Dolores, who stuck by me and showed me God in her lifestyle. And to my wife Valerie who, in my adult years, was instrumental in bringing me to God.

Contents

Foreword

$\mathcal{J}$ have been intimately involved in martial arts for more than five decades. I feel honored to be one of Grandmaster Ed Parker's first generation black belts and to have studied privately with Bruce Lee for many years.

I first heard the name Donnie Williams in the early 1970s. He had a reputation of an arrogant black man who was making a mark for himself on the karate tournament circuit. Interviews of Williams showcased a powerful warrior fueled by fierce racial hatred. Because I was a prominent white man schmoozing with top Hollywood celebrities and married to a superstar, I wasn't overly eager to meet the likes of Donnie Williams, and in fact didn't for many years.

In February 2001 I worked on a book with Tom Bleecker called *The Journey: the Oral Histories of the Most Proficient American Kenpoists of Today,* which had a fast-track publication date of August 2001. Essentially this book chronicled the journeys of two dozen karate masters residing in America. It came as no surprise that Grandmaster Donnie Williams was included as one of the 24 esteemed honorees.

Early on, Tom and I agreed that our biggest obstacle was going to be the egos of these martial arts luminaries. Although we set stringent guidelines, we anticipated many might want to use this book to glorify, and even reinvent, themselves. Above all else, we felt that none of the honorees would want to be portrayed in the book as being on the lower rungs of the totem pole and would do all in their power to avert such an implication. With this in mind, we scheduled what we predicted would be the most difficult interviews last. Grandmaster Donnie Williams was placed on this list.

While attempting to schedule an interview with Williams, I learned through the Black Karate Federation that Grandmaster Williams was more appropriately referred to as Bishop Donnie Williams and that I should contact him through The Family Church in Pasadena where he was the senior pastor. Wonderful. Besides martial arts, religion was now in the mix. Days later I worked my way through the church theocrats and arranged a specific time to conduct a one-hour telephone interview.

On the day I called Bishop Williams, and following our pleasant but generic greeting, he answered all my questions thoughtfully and calmly, and made no demands or suggestions with regard to embellishing his individual profile. At the conclusion of our conversation, I told him that I would be writing a first draft, which I would forward to him in a few days for his review. He thanked me and hung up. It just seemed all too easy.

Days later I sent Williams my first draft and, when I didn't hear back, quickly forgot about him. The book was now ten days from publication and, as Tom and I had anticipated, our phones were ringing constantly. Over the past month, many of the honorees had read drafts of other honoree profiles and in the eleventh hour were vying for position. Some wanted glorified war stories inserted into their profiles. Others had found better photographs that they wanted to swap for photographs already locked into the book's design. I felt like I was in the middle of a battle of a thousand samurai swords. I wasn't eating properly and was losing sleep. My wife had turned cold and the family dog ignored me.

The following morning I walked out to my office, which was detached from the main house. My wife Lisa had just placed the morning newspaper on my desk and was leaving to run errands.

"Oh, there's a call on your machine from Bishop Williams," she said.

The mere mention of his name sent a chill up my spine. "Really? What did he want?"

"I don't know. I just heard him leave his name as I came in."

I walked over to my desk and sagged into my chair. The red light on my answering machine was blinking. I took a deep breath and hit the play button, convinced that Williams hated my first draft and would have a laundry list of complaints.

"This is Bishop Donnie Williams," the message began with a deep, noncommittal drone. "I am just calling to let you know that I think you did a wonderful job on the draft you sent, and to thank you for what you've done for me and my family, and the others in the book. There is no other purpose for this call other than to say thank you." Click.

I was stunned. Lisa was impressed and said, "This Bishop sounds like someone you should take the time to meet."

Later that afternoon I called Bishop Williams and thanked him for the thoughtful message he'd left on my answering machine. I'd not forgotten Lisa's suggestion that I personally meet the Bishop. "I've got to fly to Las Vegas for the book's debut in two weeks," I said as I glanced at my desk calendar, "But when I get back, I'm coming to your church on Sunday to personally shake your hand. And not only that, I'm planning to sing, pray, and put in the basket."

There was a brief silence, followed by the Bishop's signature monotone drone, "I'll expect you. God bless." Click.

I hung up the phone and looked blankly around the room, then blurted out, "Why on earth did you tell him that? What was wrong with just taking the man to lunch? Now you've talked yourself into some black church!"

On the first Sunday following my return from Las Vegas I drove to The Family Church in Pasadena. There were a few hundred black people converging on the building, and more cars arriving. I parked on the street, straightened my tie and headed into God only knew what.

As I entered the front lobby, a man walked up to me and said, "Mr. Hyams? Bishop Williams would like for you to join him in his office." I thanked the man and followed him through the main lobby and down several hallways. Notably absent were the militant blacks known to surround Williams during his fighting years and his heyday as one of the founders of the notorious Black Karate Federation.

As I entered the office, the Bishop stood from behind his desk. I was immediately struck by his physical presence. At a trim 220 lb. and standing over six feet, he appeared bigger than life. He shook my hand, displaying a cavalier smile and piercing dark eyes, and embraced me like a long lost brother. We talked privately for ten minutes, mostly about his church and his ministering to the surrounding impoverished and drug ridden black community. With the service about to begin, he ended by saying, "Joe, I'm the happiest I've ever been. I am finally at peace with myself after all those years of being filled with racial hatred."

I was absolutely convinced of his sincerity. This was not the racist monster I had read about decades earlier. In fact there was little, if any, semblance between "Donnie Williams, 1977 World Karate Champion," and the present-day "Bishop Donnie Williams, Senior Pastor of The Family Church."

I left the Bishop's office and took a seat in the main sanctuary. The two-hour service that followed was both electrifying and spellbinding. Loved and admired by his congregation, his wife, and his children, Williams displayed a profound knowledge of the *Word* of God, while his charisma and spirituality were those of an anointed *man* of God. This was truly a radically transformed man, one who was at total peace with himself, with God, and with the human race. Something deep inside me wanted to know how and why this had happened. I believe that this book offers a compelling answer.

jh

PART ONE

My Life Story

chapter one

Savannah, Georgia 1956

$\mathcal{I}$t was the dead of winter, and the temperature was falling rapidly. I sat on our rickety porch, watching the pouring rain and listening to the gale-like winds that were blowing across the Atlantic. It was a scary place for a nine-year-old. Beyond the porch was pitch dark, but my eyes were focused on a distant opening in the woods where I hoped my momma would soon appear. She was already an hour late.

The front door to the house was slightly ajar, and I could see my 11-year-old brother Marion sitting beside my 13-year-old sister Joerene. I had another older brother named Ernest, but he had a different father and lived with another family, although I saw him often. Marion and Joerene were huddled in front of our pot-bellied stove, talking about nothing in particular and trying to stay warm. I watched Marion stoke the fire with several pieces of wood that we'd earlier that day stripped off a recently abandoned house that was adjacent to the nearby railroad tracks.

"Shut that door, Donnie! You're letting the cold air in!" Marion yelled.

"I gotta go!" I replied, as I tightened my legs together.

Joerene laughed. "So you keep telling us. You know where the toilet is."

We had an outhouse near the edge of the woods. I hated using it, especially at night because it was often visited by rats and snakes.

"I don't want to go by myself. It's dark out there."

"Good, so no one will see you. Best of all, we won't see you!"

Marion chuckled, and then threw a piece of wood at the door to scare me.

"You better stop that, Marion, or I'm telling Momma!"

"You do that," Marion fired back, "after you tell her you peed in your britches."

The three of us laughed. This playful banter kept us from worrying about Momma whenever she was late, which was often. A bolt of lightening suddenly lit up the sky, followed by pounding thunder.

"Holy Jesus!" I yelled out, and then wrapped myself tighter into the quilt I'd draped around me. It was my own personal quilt that Momma made, and each of us kids had one. Momma would take a couple of old shirts and a few pair of pants that were beyond fixing or too small for anyone to wear and cut them up into small squares. Then she'd sew them together and fill the finished product with cotton to make a quilt. Because staying warm was a high priority during the Savannah winters, she worked on several quilts throughout the year.

"What time is it, Joerene?" I yelled through the opening in the doorway.

"Time for you to get a watch!" Joerene replied.

"That's not funny, Joerene. I'm telling."

"It's five minutes to eight," she said without laughing. My sister knew that when I got mad, I'd tell on everybody, and probably because I was the youngest, Momma always listened to me.

Momma always walked or rode the bus everywhere. Even with three bus transfers, she should have been home. The rain wasn't letting up, and I hoped that she'd finished the coat she'd been working on and was wearing it. Momma made all of her own clothes, including her jacket and sweater. She didn't much care how they looked, as long as they were sturdy and warm.

As I focused my eyes back on the opening in the woods, the ground began shaking. Moments later, the Union Pacific train roared by, causing the entire house to shake. The sound of its horn coupled with its steel wheels rolling on steel tracks was deafening. That train never slowed down, and we all knew that it would kill anything that got in its way.

Just when I thought the porch couldn't get any scarier, I spotted the thin ray of light from Momma's flashlight appearing in the opening in the woods.

"Momma!" I yelled as I bolted off the porch and ran through the rain to greet her, throwing my arms around the bottom of her wet coat.

"Hello, child," she said with a smile, happy to finally be home. "How's my baby?"

"I have to go to the bathroom, Momma," I replied, jumping in place. "Can you come with me?"

"Why, of course, child. Momma be happy to."

Minutes later, we were all gathered in the kitchen where Momma had placed her big purse that more resembled a carpetbag. My brother and sister and I waited impatiently for her to remove her coat, and then I asked, "What's for dinner, Momma?"

"The Lord done blessed us tonight, child," she said as she opened her purse and removed its contents. "A nice piece of cornbread and some leftover pork from tomorrow's lunch. Mr. Simmons was quite generous this evening."

Mr. Simmons was Momma's boss at the school cafeteria where she worked in the kitchen. He occasionally gave our mother food when he felt that she'd work especially hard, which she always did. Together with a glass of Kool Aid sweetened with Karo syrup, it was going to be a nice dinner. Later, Momma would lie down with all of us in our bed until we fell asleep. Because I was the youngest, I usually got to lie beside Momma. I was greatly relieved that I was off that porch and that she was once again finally home.

My family lived in an area of Savannah, Georgia called Liberty City where 20 crudely-built houses lined several dirt streets that were often muddy. Our home was a weather-beaten two-room shack that was built on stilts to protect it from the often-overflowing banks of the Savannah River and was without running water, phone, or electricity. Our mailbox was about a half mile away.

Near the house was a pump that I loved to operate whenever Momma needed water. Like most others in our neighborhood, we had a series of tubs that were used for various purposes. A number one tub was about the size of a bucket that we used for washing our feet. The number two tub was bigger and was the one Momma used, along with her washboard, to clean our clothes. Our number three tub was specifically for baths that we took once a week— usually on Sunday before church. The biggest was the number four tub, which was used for livestock. Few black people owned this tub because, with rare exception, blacks weren't allowed to own farm animals.

When I attended grade school in the 1950s, all the schools in Georgia were segregated. Along with my brother and sister, I attended Florence Street School, which was a square three-story building made of dirty brick with an adjacent playground of cracked asphalt and dirt. We walked five miles to school and left home before dawn in order be in class by eight o'clock. It wasn't uncommon for us to make that trek through a driving rain, and by the time I arrived at school I was cold and wet. And I'd stay that way for an hour because my classroom had only a measly steam heater.

Because our all-black school was poorly funded and under-staffed, the quality of education was far below the national level. Few lawmakers cared about the futures of black kids because we weren't destined to become bank tellers and grocery store clerks, let alone doctors and lawyers. Our future was as agricultural laborers. Those who didn't end up working the plantation fields repaired railroad tracks or hauled rocks. Teaching black kids how to read and write was a low priority. The vast majority of white taxpayers cared only that we were taught to say "Yessuh" and "Yes, ma'am."

My classroom had no real amenities, just a couple dozen rickety desks, a blackboard, chalk, and a teacher whose real job was child care. I went to school because my momma made me go. I wasn't being sent to school to learn, and I knew that from the day Momma registered me.

Throughout my childhood, I was often sick and, as a result, was puny and couldn't fight. I did, however, have my brother Marion, who was two years older. If someone gave me trouble, I'd go get my brother and he'd beat the kid's head in. I often bragged about my brother's toughness and warned the kids not to mess with me. The seeds of male intimidation through violence—threatened or real—were sewn in my early years.

If there was an upside to school, it was that I loved the playground and looked forward to recess. By the end of my first semester, I developed a knack for humor and had become the school clown. Gaining people's attention by making them laugh caused me to feel special, and I became a master of everything from one-liners to pratfalls, and occasionally threw in a practical joke or two. When I'd get someone to laugh, I didn't feel unimportant and unnoticed.

I never had toys as a child. Even the simplest toys like Jacks or a Slinky were a luxury not afforded to poor black kids. Occasionally, I'd see white kids with a bicycle or a pair of key skates, but usually at a distance, and from "my side" of the street. Although my siblings and I didn't have bikes and key skates, at an early age we learned the meaning of "necessity is the mother of invention."

While the privileged kids had Savannah's beaches and municipal pools, we swam in the mud holes that remained year round from the rains and the overflow from the Savannah River. A half mile from the house and adjacent to the railroad tracks was a fishing hole, which was also the swimming hole where I hung out with my peers. We dove off a makeshift diving board and swung on an old tire that we tied to a tree with a rope. This muddy wasteland was a far cry from the beautiful Savannah River that Georgia's famous resident lyricist Johnny Mercer wrote about in "Moon River."

Although my siblings and I didn't have much, we were big time. During the summer, my brother and I made rafts from scrap wood and floated around the flooded streets and fishing holes like modern day Huck Finns and Tom Sawyers. No one could say anything to us—that is, as long as we stayed on our side of the tracks.

After years of living under the segregation of the Deep South, I felt that I'd been isolated from the rest of the American society and was living in a small microcosm of Georgia. While it was rare that I traveled outside the boundaries of Liberty City, when I did, I often felt as if I were an outcast or an untouchable.

At an early age I learned to walk in the street so that white people could walk on the sidewalks. Although I never had enough money to attend any of Savannah's movie theaters, I was told that coloreds sat in the black only balcony, and that if I were riding the bus there, I was to sit in the rear seats. When I was thirsty, I drank from black only drinking fountains. Most of all, my momma taught me to always smile politely at white people and to address them by sir and ma'am.

As a result, I came to dislike white people because I felt inferior to them. It wasn't anything they said. It was their existence. I could see that they lived in better homes, drove nicer cars, ate in better restaurants, and wore fancier clothes. No one ever told me that whites were bad people. The distinction wasn't one of good and bad. The distinction was us and them, and the strong implication that whites were better than blacks.

Everything about my life was under the control of this white power structure, including my thoughts. The worst part was this system never rewarded blacks who behaved properly, only punished those who didn't. No one ever praised me for walking in the street or drinking from the black only fountain. I never heard a thank you from anyone. No one ever told me that if I did everything right that I would receive a plaque for the best colored kid in Liberty City. Out of fear, I whistled in the dark and lived with the sense of waiting for the other shoe to drop. Perhaps living in poverty and being segregated from the mainstream of the American society wouldn't have been so bad if every now and then I had received even the least amount of praise—but I never did.

All was not lost. By the mid-1950s the popularity of television began to open my eyes to the outside world. Although we didn't have electricity in our home, one of the families in our neighborhood did. They had a small television with rabbit ears that worked well enough to receive two of the major network stations being broadcast out of Savannah. Thankfully, ten-year-old Jeremy was one of the kids in that family, and Jeremy and I were friends.

Beginning around the age of ten, I'd walk down to Jeremy's house and sit on the sofa with him while we watched TV and drank lemonade and ate cookies. I would sit spellbound as I watched shows like "I Love Lucy," "Ozzie and Harriet," and "Father Knows Best." Even though the stars of those programs were white, I didn't care because I was so overwhelmed by the world they were living in. Where was this place? Was it on some other planet? And where was "Disneyland"? And who were these child "Mouseketeers" who belonged to this special club?

One afternoon I saw a show called "The Price Is Right." I couldn't believe what I was seeing as I watched the emcee give away an ice box—actually gave it away for free! I turned to Jeremy and pointed at the television. "Jeremy, did you see that? That guy just gave that woman a free ice box!"

Jeremy kept munching cookies, unimpressed. "Naw. They just do that on TV. They're just acting."

"Acting? Jeremy, that lady ain't acting. She's a housewife with a bunch of kids. That's what she said."

"Go ahead and believe it if you want," Jeremy replied with a chuckle.

"Hey, I'm telling you she just got a free ice box!"

Later in the show, a contestant won a car, which was all I could take. Jeremy and I got to yelling so loudly at each other that his mother finally shooed me out of the house. On my walk home I still couldn't believe what I'd seen. Where were these shows, and how in the world could they afford to give away all those expensive prizes? They must all be millionaires. I wanted to be a part of that. I wanted to be like them. Somehow I got the impression that they all lived in California.

After nearly a year of watching TV at Jeremy's house, I decided that I truly wanted to be—and needed to be—somebody. I had no future in Georgia where few people besides my family cared one iota about me. I wasn't going to spend the rest of my life imprisoned in Liberty City and isolated from the rest of society when I hadn't done anything wrong except for being born with dark skin.

It was around this time that I started dressing up. I'd put on a white T-shirt and tied a tie around my neck. A lot of people thought I looked ridiculous, but I didn't care. To me, I looked successful like those actors I saw on TV. Ozzie Nelson always wore a tie, even at the dinner table. When I wore that T-shirt and tie, I felt like Mr. Nelson and the others. That tie made me feel important, and I'd occasionally wear it to dinner.

Marion would laugh, but I wouldn't let him get to me. "One day I'm going to be rich, Marion. You'll see. I'm going to have a real swimming pool in my backyard. I'm going to be special and have lots of friends. And I'm not going to be walking in the street or floating around on a raft. I'm going to be driving around Savannah in one of them big, fancy Cadillac cars. People are going to look close when Donnie Williams drives through town."

In the fall of 1959, when I was 12 years old, I started being drawn to the hoboes who hung around the railroad tracks. Unlike what I saw on TV, I didn't want to look like them. Most were dirty and unshaven and smelled of alcohol and cigarettes. Many were toothless. Yet, I was captivated by their stories. They appeared in Georgia during the spring and fall. When the hot and humid summers or the bitter cold winters became unbearable, they'd pull up stakes, jump the rails, and head for more comfortable climates. More than any other place, these hoboes liked to spin yarns about California, and their descriptions closely resembled what I'd been seeing on television.

chapter two

Joe Williams

When I was a young boy growing up in Savannah in the 1950s, it was rare that anyone, especially my mother, talked about my father. I never knew much about my father's family background other than the fact that his name was Joe Williams and that he had a brother named Pledge. It was strange growing up in a family where no one, including the mother, talked about the father of three of the family's four children.

Around the time I was finishing grade school, I visited my Aunt Mildred at her home in Pembroke, Georgia where my momma was born and raised. Mildred was a kind woman who seemed to feel sorry for my loss. One afternoon when we were sitting alone together on the porch, I asked her, "Mildred, tell me something. Who was my father? Where did he come from?"

She looked out at the road that ends at her house, and after a moment said, "Years ago your momma and me was sitting on this same porch, just like you and me are now, when this tall, handsome man come around that corner from out of nowhere and just swooped your momma off her feet. And your momma was no more the same—and she left Pembroke and went to Savannah with him."

Most of the kids in Liberty City had fathers who lived with them. It was considered almost a sin or a curse for a family not to have a husband and wife living in the same home. The two could hate each other, but they stayed together to raise children.

In the 1940s it was common for girls in their teens to be giving birth, but my momma was in her early twenties when she began having children. My father, who was 30 years her senior, was 55 years old when I was born. He wasn't present when my mother gave birth because a week earlier he'd left home one morning to tend to his whiskey making business and was never seen or heard from again.

From what little I could gather, my father was originally from Alabama and a gambler by trade. In the late 1930s, he came with my mother to Liberty city where he held a number of menial jobs, although eventually his main source of income came from supplying bootleg whiskey to the locals.

It was rumored around Liberty City that Joe Williams had a prison mentality. There was a general sense that he was running, and wherever he was running to and running from, no one knew. Back in the 1940s in the Deep South, if a man got into trouble and was sent to prison—especially a black man—when he got out, he was running for the rest of his life. If my momma knew whether or not my father had spent time in prison, she never talked about it.

My father was born in 1892, not long after the enactment of what became known in the Deep South as the Black Codes and Jim Crow laws.

Shortly after the Civil War, white Southerners moved quickly to eliminate black people's newfound freedom and return them to their prewar status as slaves. Around that time, minstrel shows had become popular. One particular show featured a character named Jim Crow who was played by white actors in black make-up known as "black face." Named after this character, these harsh laws restricted the freedom of black people from the 1880s to the 1960s.

Signs that said "Whites Only" or "Colored" were displayed at entrances to railways and streetcars, public waiting rooms, restaurants, boardinghouses, theaters, and public parks. Separate schools, hospitals, and other public institutions, generally of inferior quality, were designated for blacks. Prisons and child reform schools were also segregated. No colored barber was allowed to cut the hair of white women or girls. Blacks weren't allowed to shoot pool with whites, and it was unlawful for any amateur colored baseball team to play baseball in any vacant lot or baseball diamond within two blocks of any playground devoted to the white race. Even in death, blacks were not permitted to be buried in the same cemetery as whites.

Beginning in the early 1950s when I was around the age of six, I began experiencing a recurring dream that began with my searching for my father in the woods that were adjacent to our house. In the dream I walked through the woods and came upon a cleared out area where I saw my father in the distance. He was dressed in overalls and a white shirt, and stood over a large barrel that was suspended over a fire with hoses running everywhere and piles of corn mash nearby. I called out to him several times, but he either didn't hear me or chose not to hear me. In the dream, I had the unsettling feeling that he didn't want anything to do with me. Then just when I was overcome with the urge to run to him, a group of angry men appeared suddenly from out of the woods. Then the dream would quickly change to another location where my father was running, and I could hear the sound of barking dogs and gunshots. In the morning, I'd awaken with mixed feelings. On the one hand I felt scared because I dreamt that my father had been killed, while on the other hand I felt relieved because whenever I experienced this dream, it began with him being alive.

I was angry about my father being gone and, because of the life I'd been living, eventually blamed white men for his disappearance. Those barking dogs in my dream were the same dogs that had hunted down runaway slaves. And the men that hunted those slaves were white men, who found and shot the slaves, lynched them, or returned them to owners, who whipped them and bound them in chains. Black people didn't hunt blacks, white men did.

Whether lawmen or poachers, white people were also the ones who went looking for clandestine whiskey stills, and when they found stills, there was often trouble. If my father did have a prison record, he most likely would've run, and the white men wouldn't have hesitated to shoot him.

Or maybe my father was just in the wrong place at the wrong time. During the 1940s, black people were highly discouraged from entering towns in which they didn't reside. In order to keep food on the table, maybe my father had to deliver his bootlegged whiskey to a distant town where he was questioned and thrown in jail. The authorities wouldn't have felt obliged to inform his wife about his incarceration, and when my father eventually got out, he may have just thought it best not to return home. At 55, he had to have been physically and emotionally tired from living a lifetime of oppression. Awakening each day with an empty feeling of hopelessness must have worn heavily on him.

Of course, the nature of his whiskey business and the notion that he'd spent time in prison would have resulted in his being associated with scores of seedy characters. Maybe one of them, or a group of them, caught up with him to settle an old score or to take over his still. Or maybe … or maybe … or maybe … after a while it didn't matter. Whatever happened to my father, in my mind it wasn't good, and one way or another I blamed white people. Whichever theory was correct, or if none of them were, the cold, hard reality was that I often felt like my father was dead, and he was never coming back.

Not having a father at home was hard on me, and a day didn't go by that I wasn't reminded of this in one form or another. I'd be down at the fishing hole with the guys, and one of the old geezers would threaten some kid for making too much noise and scaring away the fish. The kid would yell back, "I'm gonna go tell my papa and he's gonna come down here and whup you!" And a couple of times that's exactly what happened. Or kids would proudly say, "When I grow up, I want to be just like my papa." Or I'd see their fathers playing stick ball with them, or wrestling with them, or swimming. I didn't have a father to do those things with me, which hurt and often made me feel alone.

Although I didn't have a father at home, I allowed myself to get close to a man who became a father figure to me. His name was Bishop Owens, my momma's pastor. He was a physically strong man who was always smiling and had an abundance of energy.

When I went to church with my momma, I didn't pay attention to much of what was said, except when Bishop Owens spoke because he talked a lot about the importance of family and keeping the family together. All the kids loved him because he always had time for us, and when he had an extra 50 cents, he'd buy us candy. Throughout the year, he'd arrange a family potluck at the church and special events for the kids like Halloween night. And he never forgot any of our birthdays and would make a point of wishing us happy birthday during the church service.

The bishop was aware of my not having a father at home and regularly asked my mother how her kids were doing. Whenever she had a problem that was too much for her to handle, she'd call the bishop and he'd come to the house to help. In my heart, I eventually accepted him as part of our family and the closest thing I had to a father, which helped relieve the painful void I had in my life.

Then one afternoon I came home from the fishing hole, and my momma told me that Bishop Owens had died. To this day I can't recall my initial reaction, except that I stood in the middle of the room, physically frozen and emotionally in shock. I didn't ask how he died because I didn't want to know. I went to bed that night and quietly cried myself to sleep. The only real thing that mattered to me was that Bishop Owens was dead, and he was never coming back.

chapter three

Lissie

My mother was born in Savannah-Pembroke in the summer of 1922 and was given the birth name Lissie Kent. Her parents were extremely poor. Although it's difficult to verify our family lineage, it's believed that my mother's maternal great-grandparents, Clarence and Mary Rawls, were slaves.

Momma wasn't an educated woman, although she attended Chester High School and completed the seventh grade. Unlike many black women living in the Deep South in the 1940s, she could read and write.

Over the years, religion became my momma's way of consoling the pain of prejudice and oppression. Beginning in early childhood, her hope came from the black clergymen who stood in the pulpits of Southern Baptist and Holiness churches each Sunday preaching God's promise of salvation. She placed no importance on people's physical appearance, where they lived, or how much money they had. To her, all that mattered was their relationship with the Lord. With each breath my momma took, she lived to serve God and accepted death as a natural occurrence of returning home to the Father. As early back as I can remember, she often said, "Son, when the Lord comes, I'm waiting on Him. When He comes to get me, I'm ready to go."

My mother was taught from an early age to believe that poverty was a good thing. The church told her that she was rich with salvation, that she didn't need money, and that all she'd ever need in life was Jesus. Because of this mindset, she never worried about a paycheck. She'd work all week, and if she didn't need to buy groceries, the paycheck wouldn't be important. My momma would make 40 dollars a week, and four dollars would go to the church. Even if the rent was due or she had no money for Christmas, she never failed to tithe 10 percent of everything she earned.

Besides tithing, if she felt that the pastor needed something, she'd go to the other women in the church and fight for him. "Pastor Owens needs a new suit," I overheard her say one Sunday to a group of churchwomen. "He's been wearing that same suit each week for a year. Let's get him a new one because he's a man of God. I know he didn't ask us, but let's buy him one."

Momma accepted her role as an obedient, mild-mannered woman of God. The church taught her not only to be submissive in life, but to be submissive in her marriage, and she could quote chapter and verse from the Bible that showed where God had instructed her to be submissive to her husband. Men loved my momma's submissiveness and her belief that it was her duty to serve them. Her submissiveness and total devotion to God wasn't unique to my mother. All the women of the church were this way.

Besides working long hours in the kitchen of the community's all-black school, my mother worked as a domestic in the homes of lower class white families. When she worked as a domestic, she never entered the home of a white family through the front door. She could go to their front door once she was inside the house, but on her initial arrival she was required to always enter through the back door. And when she left, she left through the back door.

Whatever it took, Momma made certain that I and my siblings never went to bed hungry. When the Savannah River wasn't overflowing, she planted vegetables in a small garden patch and raised her own chickens year round. She made good use of the eggs and occasionally slaughtered one of the chickens to put food on the table. When the flood waters were down, she placed raw chicken necks into tin cans and lowered them down from the porch as bait for crawfish. A staple dish in our home was Hoppin' John, which was an old slave recipe of rice, red peas, and smoked hog jowl. When times were really tough, she cooked up a couple of blackbirds that a neighbor would give her.

My momma was a firm believer in the old saying "Spare the rod and spoil the child," and she'd spank us kids for just about anything. The worst part was that she'd never forget. She'd catch me chewing gum in church on Sunday, and then the following Tuesday she'd suddenly appear in front of me and say, "I haven't forgotten about you chewing gum in church last Sunday! Go outside and get a switch!" Other times she'd slap us right there in church. My momma was a strict woman who didn't stand for any guff.

By the same token, she was loving and fair. After being punished, I'd crawl up into her arms and she would love and comfort me. My siblings and I looked forward to sitting in her lap, even when we were big. At any given time, and often for no particular reason, she'd say to me, "You're my baby. C'mon over here, baby. C'mon over here and sit in Momma's lap." Then she'd rock me and sing to me, sometimes until I fell asleep.

I always knew where I stood with my mother. When I did something good, she'd pull me in and talk to me and hug me. And if I did something wrong, I'd hear about it on no uncertain terms. Because of her positive attitude and her strong faith in God, she constantly reassured me that I could make something of my life, and often told me, "You're gonna make it, son. You're gonna do it, boy. That's my baby. He's gonna do it."

I hated that my mother worked so hard for such a meager salary. She made just enough to get by and had no insurance, savings, or benefits of any kind. After working a full day, she'd come home and fix dinner, and then catch up on whatever chores needed to be done. It was only after she'd put her kids to bed that she'd sit on our worn out sofa and read her Bible. There were nights that I would peek at her from the adjacent room and see her leaning beside her kerosene lamp, squinting to read through the cheap pair of glasses she bought on sale at the local dime store. It saddened me to see her broken down shoes on the floor and her tired feet resting inside our number one tub filled with heated water. In the early morning hours, she'd close her Bible, and then her eyes, only to get up the next morning and disappear again through that small opening in the woods.

I felt that my momma deserved a better life and wished that there were something I could do to help her. But the truth was there wasn't anything. Even though I was approaching my teens, I was too scrawny to do hard labor, so my earning capability was in sorrier condition than hers.

Although I knew that finding another husband would make my mother's life easier, at least financially, I didn't want her to remarry because I hadn't completely lost hope that my father would return one day. In the meantime, even though I was the youngest, and without means and couldn't fight, I still wanted my momma to feel that I'd protect her. I wanted her to see me as the man of the house. Not that she ever thought of me as her protector. She didn't need me or any other human being because she had God. The Lord was her sole protector, and she relied totally on His ability to fulfill her every need and answer her every prayer.

Regardless, I wanted to be my momma's hero, and I often said to her, "One day I'm going to be rich and I'm going to build you a big fancy house. It's going to have a big kitchen and heat and electricity and a TV, and you're going to have your own maid and be able to relax and do what you please." Momma would just smile and thank me for my well wishes and concern, and then tell me to run outside and play.

Nothing in my momma's life matched what I saw on TV. When I'd watch television at Jeremy's house, I'd see a 300-pound black lady with a rag on her head handling silver trays and serving white people in their big mansion. Now and then she'd be singing and laughing in the kitchen. She ate well and had her own room, and all the family members called her by her first name. Then I'd go home and sit with my brother and sister, shivering in front of our potbellied stove and eating ketchup sandwiches while our mother stuffed rags into the cracks of our thin-walled shack.

Around the time I turned 12, I became increasingly angry. I was angry at the people who initially enslaved us. I was angry at the white people who refused to honor our freedom from slavery by immediately enacting the Black Codes and Jim Crow laws that dishonored the courage and bravery of every solider who fought in the Civil War. I was angry at the church for teaching my mother to be submissive and for making her believe that poverty was a good thing. And I was angry at God—yes, God—for allowing it all to happen.

As I grew older, I came to recognize that my momma's faith was always stronger than any obstacle she ever faced in life. Through all the hardship she endured, I never once heard her cuss, let alone complain. She was a positive woman, almost to a fault, and her faith was unyielding. She accepted life on life's terms because she believed that life's terms were God's terms.

chapter four

First Christ Holiness Church of Savannah

Ly mother instilled my faith in God at an early age. She was devoted to the First Christ Holiness Church of Savannah, and every Sunday, rain or shine, our family walked three miles to Sunday services.

I didn't look forward to Sundays because I hated the way I looked. Momma made all of our clothes, except for those she acquired from the church. When our clothes got torn, she'd sew them up and put patches on them. She would suddenly show up with one of my older brother's worn dress shirts and slip it on me.

I'd look down at the cuffs and could barely see my fingernails. "Momma, what is this?"

"Never mind, child. We're late."

"No, wait. I can't wear this. It's too big."

She'd ignore me and begin rolling up the sleeves. "It fit just fine. Put a nice bowtie on and—"

"A bowtie! No, Momma. Let me wear my T-shirt under the jacket and a regular tie!"

"You ain't wearin' no T-shirt to church! I taught you better!" Then she'd smack me on the head. "Now, child, don't start up!" She'd button up the shirt and clip on a bowtie that fell three inches below the bottom of my neck.

I'd quietly whine as she rolled up my pant legs, showing the ragged seams. When the jacket got put on, the sleeves hung to my knuckles.

My brother would pass by, pausing just long enough to comment, "You look nice, Donnie … for a clown." He'd walk off chuckling to himself, and I'd start yelling. We'd go through this every Sunday until I grew into those clothes.

Besides my hand-me-down clothes, I walked those three miles in a pair of ugly shoes. The soles were thin flaps that were held together by clothes hanger wire. They didn't have shoelaces and were a mishmash of gray and brown, even though everyone referred to them as my black shoes. And those were my good shoes, my Sunday shoes. The worst part was that those ugly hand-me-down shoes were actually given to me on Christmas as a gift!

Our congregation amounted to about 30 members. We met in a small run-down structure that had a dirt floor covered with sawdust. Prior to the service, two older women would beat big round drums that could be heard from a half-mile off. In addition to the drums, several members played scrub boards to accompany the congregation's singing, which was so loud it could raise the roof. More than the preacher's message, it was the singing that drew the people to church. I'd sit beside my mother, spellbound as I watched her come alive with shouts of "Hallelujah! Praise God!" as she looked heavenward while waving her arms overhead. An hour into the service, members would "catch fire" as the Holy Spirit came upon them, shaking involuntarily as if having seizures. They'd shake and contort and often fall to the ground in a trance. Nearby members would rush to them and fan them with towels. Many often spoke in unknown tongues. Healings, sometimes miraculous, were common.

During the 1950s, televangelists of the Rex Humbard, Oral Roberts, Benny Hinn, and Billy Graham ilk were becoming popular, and white preachers and evangelists were starting to be welcomed into the black churches because black preachers were considered less educated. Black preachers would hold up the Bible during their sermons, but for many it was merely a prop. Their sermons were simple and spoken—often shouted—from the heart. My momma felt that if a preacher didn't become soaked with perspiration and winded from strutting and hoarse from shouting the Word of God, then he hadn't done his best. She would've gotten along well with President Lincoln, who once remarked, "When I see a man preach, I like to see him act as if he were fighting bees."

In the minds of black people, preachers were called by God, and their congregation had to believe what emanated from their mouths because it was believed that God spoke to them directly. In sharp contrast, however, most white ministers were seminary graduates and because of this were treated with more respect. Blacks tended to listen more intensely to white preachers because academically white preachers understood the written Word of God.

When I was around 11, Pastor Owens was an hour into his Sunday sermon when everyone suddenly became aware of a man standing in the open main doorway. James Vaughn was dressed in a neatly pressed white suit and had a large Bible tucked under his arm. He was a reasonably good looking man who had a presence about him. Pastor Owens paused in his sermon as we turned our collective gaze toward this man perusing the congregation. Bright sunlight cast an almost heavenly glow around him. All that was missing were singing angels.

When he finally entered, he informed us that the Lord had sent him to run a revival. It didn't take long for Preacher Vaughn to talk Bishop Owens into allowing him to hold his revival. The following Sunday, Vaughn delivered a fiery sermon to a packed, captivated house. But his thoughts were more on my momma—whom he had marked as a passionately devoted woman of God and a single woman with four children—than on God having sent him as His messenger.

James Vaughn was a vagabond who traveled throughout the South looking for a place to call home, and my mother gave him that opportunity by allowing him to call on her. When he began calling on my mother, Georgia was still vehemently segregated.

In the South during the '50s whites avoided contact with coloreds, and we harbored the same bias, distancing ourselves from the whites who showed us no respect. Unless they were salesmen, white men didn't call on black homes. They got their money and quickly went about heir business.

Vaughn broke this barrier, and he got away with it because both blacks and whites afforded white preachers a degree of tolerance because it was sometimes necessary for a white preacher to go to a black home to minister to the sick or pray with the family over a tragedy. But this was still a fine line. Once the ministering was over, white preachers were expected to leave, which Vaughn didn't do. Instead, he began staying for dinner.

One of the strongest taboos in the South was based on the Jim Crow law that whites and blacks were never to eat together. I always knew when Vaughn was expected because my momma would set an extra place at our dinner table.

He would wait up the road until there was no one around and then hurriedly slip into our house and close the door. Along with my brother and sister, I didn't like this because I knew that his presence at dinner was eventually going to become a problem.

After Vaughn would leave, my mother would sit on the porch with me and my siblings. It was as if a spell had come over her. I'd never known her to appear so naïve. No matter how much I and my brother and sister objected to this white preacher, she staunchly defended him, telling us that he was an anointed man of God.

I hated Vaughn and didn't want him to be with my mother. I didn't like his controlling nature or the way he talked down to me, and I especially didn't like him because he was white. I may have lived in a shack that sat on stilts, but it was my shack, not his.

It wasn't long before my worst nightmare came true. One night after dinner, Vaughn told my mother that God had told him that she was going to be his wife. Because she honestly felt that this preacher was a true man of God, she believed him.

I wasn't the only kid in Liberty City who didn't want white men to be with black women. None of my friends liked the idea of Vaughn seeing my mother. At school my classmates began making fun of me, and I was even cursed at. I personally blamed Vaughn and wished he were dead. If I never saw another white man for the rest of my life, it wouldn't be soon enough.

Over time the church elders saw Vaughn for what he was—a fast-buck evangelist traveling across the country using God to separate believers from their money. This white preacher wasn't serving God; he was using God to line his own pockets. He was snake oil—get the money and move on, and all in the name of Jesus.

These elders began to pressure my mother to end the relationship. They came to our home and quoted from the Bible where it warns vulnerable women about ill-intentioned men who can creep into their lives and take them captive. My mother listened politely, but it didn't matter. She held to her belief that Vaughn had the best of intentions and continued to defend him.

Tragedy struck our home in the early morning hours of New Year's Day, 1958. All four of us were asleep in one bed—our only bed—when Momma was awakened by a neighbor yelling from outside with shouts of "Fire! Fire!" Momma had a difficult time rousing us kids, but finally managed to awaken us and quickly ushered us from our burning house.

Regardless of the time of day or night, whenever someone shouted "Fire!" neighbors came running with their number one tubs. Within minutes they were working a bucket brigade, furiously pumping water from the single well. Ten minutes later one fire truck arrived. It was an old tanker with one round rusted tank and a man in front cranking away at the pump that resulted in a thin stream of water that did absolutely nothing. All the crying, praying, and neighbors' water brigade were unable to save our ramshackle home from the consuming flames. I stood in the cold night air in my pajamas and watched our two-room shack and what little worldly possessions we had being reduced to a smoldering pile of ashes.

I slept on the back seat of a car that night and the following morning awoke to the reality that all had been lost—my home, my fishing pole, my white T-shirt and tie, everything gone. I was no longer a poor black kid with very little. I was a poor black kid without a roof over my head. And I was barefoot—even my ugly shoes were no more.

With tears streaming down my face, I ran straight to Momma, who told me that God was going to take care of us and not to worry. Then she pulled me and my brother and sister into her and wrapped her tattered coat around us.

From that moment on, I didn't worry because I believed everything my momma said. She was my security, my guiding light, my beacon in a storm, my rock. I knew we were going to make it—because my momma said so. As long as I still had her, everything was going to be all right.

Over the next few days, my mother began collecting hand-me-downs and we stayed with a neighboring family. But it was to be only temporary. Momma had no savings, and the reality that we had no permanent place to go began to sink in.

James Vaughn took advantage of my mother's situation and boldly announced to her that the fire had been an act of God. If that wasn't bad enough, he further convinced her that God had told him that she should leave me with my sister and travel with him to Florida. Much to my utter dismay, she agreed, assuring me that she'd send for me in six months. What I would soon learn about Vaughn would cause me to hate him even more.

The Deep South was clear about its position on interracial marriage. Years earlier the Jim Crow laws had made it unlawful for a white person to marry a Negro or mulatto or person with one-eighth or more Negro blood. Moreover, whites and blacks weren't allowed to travel together. This presented a problem for Vaughn traveling with my mother to Florida, which was even deeper into the segregated South than Georgia.

To get around this, Vaughn put my mother on a bus while he hopped on a plane. Upon reuniting in Florida, Vaughn checked into a motel where he passed my mother off as his housekeeper. The thought of my momma, who was a devoted woman of God, carrying this white preacher's bags while walking behind him with her head lowered made me sick. Ultimately, Vaughn's charade didn't play well in Florida where life became worse than it had been in Savannah, and within weeks he convinced my mother to marry him and head for California.

I was now entering my teens, and in my mother's absence I became incorrigible. It didn't take long for my sister to reach her breaking point, and arrangements were made for me to travel to California to be reunited with my momma.

I had mixed emotions about going to California. Although I knew I was oppressed in Georgia and had little hope of a future, at least I knew where I stood. I understood the rules and abided by them. All I knew about California was what I saw on television and heard from the hoboes. While I was nervous about traveling into uncharted waters, I was eager to be reunited with my mother. Hopefully by the time I arrived Vaughn would be gone or in jail or dead. When my momma talked with me on the phone, she hadn't mentioned him, and I didn't ask. The night before I left Savannah, I walked to where my father's whiskey still once was and said my farewells, adding that I hoped that one day perhaps we would meet.

The next day I boarded a Trailways bus with a sack of peanut butter and jelly sandwiches, a big bag of potato chips, and two canned sodas. Over the next two days I stared out the window at the passing sights and began to feel good about having left Georgia.

By the end of the second day, it dawned on me that I'd never again see another outhouse and that soon I'd be living in a house with electricity and running water. Mail would be delivered directly to the house. No more stilts and threatening floods and walking in mud. Best of all, my momma had a telephone—and probably a television. She hadn't mentioned a swimming pool, but I guessed there was a good chance she had one. After all, I was headed for California where the black people I saw on television lived like millionaires. Maybe Vaughn was right. Maybe our shack burning to the ground was an act of God. Sunny California awaited me, and it was mine for the taking. Life out West was surely going to be a pleasant experience.

chapter five

California

When the Trailways bus arrived at its final destination in California, two things were on my mind. First, I'd finally arrived in the Land of Opportunity and was now only steps away from being installed in my mansion. By the end of the day I expected to be floating around on a rubber raft in my own private swimming pool, drinking an ice cold Pepsi. And second, that James Vaughn wouldn't be there.

When I stepped off the bus in El Monte, what I first noticed were hordes of Mexicans. I'd never seen a Mexican before because there were only two races in Georgia, white and black. Although I didn't know what to make of these people, I thought that perhaps they were the American Indians that I heard about in grade school. Anyway, none of them seemed bothered by my presence, so I paid them no mind.

Moments later I was reunited with my momma, who came to pick me up in her recently purchased used car, and headed for our new home, which was located in an area of Duarte called Rocktown. It was during the drive that she informed me that James Vaughn was still around. In fact, he was at the house waiting to welcome me home. I said nothing.

To say that Rocktown fell short of my expectations would be a gross understatement. There was good reason for this black ghetto being named Rocktown because the place was filled with rocks. At first glance it looked like one big rock quarry. There were rocks piled up everywhere. Even the fronts of the houses were rocks. Anyone who had strength enough to plant grass in the front yard had to first dig through four feet of rock in order to get to dirt. Even the streets were rocks. The roads were so bad that drivers had to slow down when entering the neighborhood. God knows how many sets of tires were ground into those rocks every year. The local tire shop probably did a record business, as did the neighborhood glass shop. With all those kids running around with nothing to do except throw rocks, it was a miracle that all the windows weren't boarded up with plywood.

The house that my mother and James Vaughn rented was an unsightly wooden structure, and as far as I was concerned the neighborhood wasn't right. Besides rocks and dirt, the whole community had only one streetlight five blocks from our house. While I fully expected a home that didn't have stilts and an outhouse, I expected more amenities, and this place was simply Georgia with rocks. If there had been a swimming pool in the backyard, it surely would have been filled with the same rocks I saw everywhere else.

By the close of the day I was installed in my tiny bedroom. While it wasn't what I'd envisioned, for the first time in my life I had my own bed and closet. That night my momma prepared a nice dinner, and I suffered through the sight of her waiting on the white preacher, who sat at the head of the table like he was king of the castle. I don't think I said ten words to him by the time I finished dessert.

In the strict sense of the word, I wasn't a true racist when I arrived in California. Although I didn't necessarily want to be around whites, I didn't hate them. From what little I was told when I lived in Savannah, my sense was that white people who lived in California were more liberal toward blacks than white people were in the Deep South, which turned out not to be entirely correct.

What differed were the laws. Unlike my treatment by whites in Georgia, white people in California didn't expect me to yield to them when I saw them approaching. I didn't have separate public restrooms and designated seating on buses and movie theaters, and no one objected to my being in the same company as whites. However, as to the collective attitude of whites toward blacks, it became immediately clear to me that I was looked upon as being inferior to whites. While blatant racial slurs, even those made in jest, were obvious, it was the long list of subtle nuances, such as poor service at integrated restaurants and white people cutting in front of me in line, that were a constant reminder of "my place." In school, white kids would get along with me in class but wouldn't sit with me at lunch.

My preconceived notion of the glamorous lifestyle blacks lived in California also turned out to be untrue. While I was sure that those black recording artists, star athletes, and the handful of successful black actors lived in mansions and drove luxury cars, none of them lived even remotely close to my neighborhood. I'd see their pictures now and then in magazines or on television, but life wasn't any different from what I experienced in Savannah. The truth was that all the blacks who were walking around in my world were in the same sorry shape that I was.

Two weeks after I arrived in California, my mother enrolled me at Duarte Junior High. I was 13 years old. When I began classes, it became clear that the substandard education I received in Savannah severely hampered my ability to do the work that was presented to me in the California school system. The fact that, except for recess, I never liked going to school resulted in my having little motivation to do whatever was necessary to become smart. Besides my teachers and counselors offering little help, because my mother had received an education that was even more substandard than mine, she didn't force me to do homework. Her main focus was always on God and the church.

My biggest difficulty was with reading. When I first opened my books, I'd never encountered such long sentences and didn't know what many of the words meant, let alone how to pronounce them. Although I could read to myself in private, reading orally in the classroom resulted in the other kids laughing at me. I'd place my finger on one word at a time, pausing for long periods and often reading things that weren't on the page. I felt like a naked kid in the town square.

This experience became a constant source of humiliation. At first, the kids thought I was being funny, but they soon figured out that I had a serious reading problem and thought I was stupid, or even worse—illiterate. In order to avoid reading, I'd clown or embarrass myself, or I'd tell the teacher that I left my book at home, or when it was about to be my turn to read, I'd suddenly ask the teacher if I could go to the bathroom. It wasn't long before I was looked upon as a disciplinary problem, and my grades began to fall.

I didn't know what to do about my reading problem, and none of my teachers or counselors offered any help. One day I decided to take the initiative and stayed after class to speak privately with one of my teachers, who happened to be white. I confided in him that I had a problem reading and asked if I could be excused from reading orally until the problem was resolved. I had no idea how that was going to happen, but that's what I asked him. The teacher looked at me and laughed. "What're you talking about? Why do you think you're in school? You're here to learn how to read. How are you supposed to learn to read if we excuse you from reading?"

I abruptly left before he asked me to leave, which I knew was forthcoming. As I walked to my next class, I felt worse. It wasn't as if I were asking for a whole lot. I knew that my grades would improve and that I'd feel better about coming to school if someone could have helped me with this problem. But no one cared. I wondered if that teacher would have ignored my simple request if I were white.

Although I never anticipated that I would have a problem with blacks, I soon realized that I was at the bottom of a pecking order. I was a black from the Deep South, which really stood out to blacks raised in California. The most glaring difference was the way I talked. Instead of saying "Yes," I'd say "Yes'um." Instead of saying, "I'll ask him," I said "I'll ass him." I called trousers and pants "britches." I didn't "carry my notebook," but "toted my notebook." The word "yesterday" sounded phonetically like "yes-ditty."

Equally problematic was that, being a Jim Crow black, I was far too respectful toward whites, whom I was taught to always address as "sir" and "ma'am." There were no exceptions. My black friends spotted this immediately and strongly suggested that I tone it down considerably.

It didn't take long for my mother to pick up on the new Donnie. One day my momma and I were ordering ice cream cones at a local 31 Flavors. When the white counterperson asked if I wanted two scoops of chocolate, I replied, "Right. Sure." We weren't two feet outside the store when my mother slapped me on the side of my head, which caused the top scoop of my ice cream cone to go sailing into the street. "What was that about 'Right. Sure'? It's 'Yes, sir.' I taught you better!" When I respectfully tried to point out that the counterperson couldn't have been older than 18, my momma said, "Don't talk back to me!" and cracked me on the other side of my head. I just couldn't win. I had become everyone's punching bag.

In the late 1950s gangs were prevalent at Duarte Junior High. Near the end of my second semester of the seventh grade, I joined the Highland Gangsters, which was named after Highland Avenue where we hung out on our bikes. We weren't serious delinquents, although we were mischievous. If we didn't like some guy, we'd get a marble and slingshot and bust his window and ride off. Every now and then one of us would steal candy from the local liquor store or swipe the bike of some guy who thought he was cool and park it in front of the house of the fattest and ugliest girl in school. If nothing else, the gang kept me occupied so that I didn't have to go home when Vaughn was there alone.

Months before I arrived in California, my momma purchased a used car and found employment as a cleaning woman. She went to work every day while Vaughn hung around the house, waiting for my mother and me to come home so that we could serve him. During the day, he did nothing but watch television and occasionally read his Bible. He never picked up after himself or offered to help with any of the chores. As far as I was concerned, he was a freeloading bum, and it bothered me that he was constantly ordering my momma to do everything from cooking his dinner to darning his socks.

I became so overwhelmed with my troubles at school and with Vaughn that I pretty much forgot about my father, and no one still had any idea what had become of him. The hope I had in Georgia that my father would appear and throw Vaughn through the front door didn't carry over to California. In my case, my absence from Georgia didn't make my heart grow fonder.

My friends at school didn't know about my white stepfather, although I wasn't sure they would have cared had they found out because interracial marriages weren't uncommon in and around Duarte. Had any of my peers learned about Vaughn, I would have referred to him as my mother's husband, but never my dad. It wouldn't have made any difference if he was God's second son. I didn't want a white man for a father, period.

As the weeks and months rolled by, Vaughn's controlling nature resulted in bolstering my racism. The idea of this white man bossing me around and telling me how to act and how to think was all too reminiscent of what I'd experienced in Georgia, and I began to hate the man with a passion. My mother was aware of the increasing tension between me and Vaughn, but because of her submissive nature, she kept her opinions to herself, although she prayed incessantly for God to intervene and bring peace to our home.

I never thought that Vaughn was a racist. He never called me a nigger or boy—and thank God he never called me son—but he was a tyrant and extremely dogmatic. Whatever he was or wasn't, I was very uncomfortable around him. He'd threatened me physically on several occasions, and I knew that if I smarted off to him, he would have whupped me, and my momma would have allowed it.

The tension came to a head one Sunday shortly after my mother left for church. She'd washed some clothes, and Vaughn told me to take the wash outside and hang it on the clothesline. I told him that he wasn't my dad, and that if my momma wanted me to hang out the wash, she would have said so before she left—and then topped it off with a couple of swear words that I knew would aggravate him. Before he could react, I left the house.

When I returned early that evening, Vaughn had already explained our entire confrontation to my mother. I had no doubt that he embellished his side, but this wouldn't have mattered because of my mother's subservience. Although she attempted to ease the tension, Vaughn silenced her and turned to me and threw down the gauntlet. First thing tomorrow morning I was to take that wash outside and hang it up.

Much to his and my mother's surprise, I refused, which provoked him into grabbing me. Vaughn was a big man, but I knew that one way or another I'd hurt him. My mother must have sensed this in me, and she stepped between us and told me to go to my room. Reluctantly I complied. I fell asleep listening to Vaughn lecturing my mother in the kitchen.

The following morning when I awoke and walked into the living room, I could instantly tell that the discussion Vaughn had the previous night with my mother hadn't gone in my favor. He sat on the living room sofa, gloating, with his hands neatly folded across his chest. Initially he gave my mother an ultimatum—either return me to Savannah to live with my sister Joerene or he would leave and their marriage would be over. In lieu of sending me back to Georgia, my mother convinced Vaughn to agree to sending me next door to live with a neighbor, an older single woman known as Miss Bess.

I was stunned. My mother had essentially been put in a no-win situation, and because of what she felt was her duty to her husband, she agreed to send me to the house next door. I moved out that same day.

Although Miss Bess was a kind woman and made every attempt to be nice to me, we didn't get along. I was furious that this white man had thrown me out of my own house, and my anger and surly attitude boiled over to her. I don't know how long we could have continued under the circumstances, but as it turned out it didn't matter. When a friend of my mother's learned about the arrangement, she went to my mother and told her that California law was very specific about parents sending their children to live with anyone who wasn't biologically related to them. If my living with Miss Bess continued, there was a chance that the Department of Social Services could find out and my mother could be in trouble.

Thus began round two, which turned out to be the final round. When my mother apprised Vaughn of what she had learned and that she had no choice but to allow me back into the home, Vaughn again demanded that she send me back to Georgia. But this was no longer a viable option because my sister had recently given birth and her home was just too hectic. It wasn't that my mother was refusing to accommodate her husband, but rather that she simply had no choice but to bring me home.

On the night I returned, and unbeknownst to my mother, Vaughn packed anything she had of value into her car and drove off in the early morning hours, never to be heard from again. The following day, my mother called the bank and learned that there was nothing left of her savings and that two days earlier her husband had personally come by the bank and closed the account.

In the weeks that followed, my momma never complained about what Vaughn had done to her. And if I'd brought it up, she would have defended him, saying that he was the man of the house and that what was hers also belonged to him. She also never complained when she was later informed that two years earlier Vaughn had arrived in Rocktown and taken up residence—with a black woman he had only recently met.

Although for a month my momma was slightly depressed, she never once blamed me for what had occurred. To her, nothing ever occurred in her life that wasn't preordained by God. To me, I was just glad the man was gone.

chapter six

Abandoning God

While I was happy that the departure of James Vaughn reunited me with my mother, it did little to alleviate my problems outside my home.

After graduating junior high school, I began attending Monrovia High. It was a shock. Compared to my grade school in Savannah, as well as my junior high school, Monrovia High was like a sprawling college campus, and I quickly felt lost.

Although in junior high my clown act had worked well in diverting attention away from the fact that I was a poor student, when I entered high school, my teachers began to label me as a classroom disturbance who was hindering the progress of serious students.

What was taking place outside the classroom wasn't any better. Unlike my classmates in Savannah, who were all black, Monrovia High was a melting pot of Hispanics, blacks, and whites. Because of my small stature and my nonaggressive nature, it wasn't long before I began to be picked on. To one degree or another I feared everyone, even some of the blacks who tended to treat me differently because I came from the Deep South.

Mexicans worried me because they ran in families that looked out for each other. Even their homes were overcrowded. It wasn't unusual for a two-bedroom house to be occupied by 15 people from several generations. Individually, as well as collectively, they responded to any threat with a pack mentality that scared me. Although when I lived in Georgia, Marion stood up for me, the few fights I did have were one on one. No one ganged up on anyone. The thought of fighting one Mexican was bad enough. The thought of fighting five was horrifying.

Because whites looked down on me as a poor black, my problem with them continued to escalate. When I lived in Georgia, this wasn't an issue because I wasn't around whites. While I knew that the whites in Savannah had a much better lifestyle than I did, I wasn't exposed to it because I lived in a black neighborhood and attended an all-black school. My exposure changed radically once I arrived in California and began attending an integrated school where the majority of whites wore nicer clothes and lived in better neighborhoods and some even drove cars—all of which I felt was being flaunted in my face. The fact that most whites had money in their pockets and targeted me with racial slurs only added to my insecurity and anxiety.

When I first entered Monrovia High, I didn't experience much aggression from the other students because a pecking order hadn't been established. It wasn't until after I became labeled as one of the weaker ones that I became a target. Bigger students purposely bumped against me in the hallways or punched me in the arm or chest. Someone would throw food at me in the cafeteria or grab my notebook and toss it under the back wheel of a departing school bus. Eventually I was spit at and beat up in the bathroom. When it became clear to me that these acts of aggression were worsening, I decided I had to do something about it.

During the mid-1960s gangs had become increasingly popular, especially to minorities. Whites tended to call their groups "clubs," which gave them an air of social acceptance like the Elks Club. But to blacks and Hispanics, these groups had the menacing title of gangs, and their members were often referred to as juvenile delinquents.

Feeling that I was in dire need of protection and acceptance, I attempted to join a local black gang in Duarte, but was turned down because I couldn't fight. Although I tried to win over the members by shoplifting cigarettes and setting fire to trash cans and other displays of courage, the group didn't want the job of protecting me in order to avoid the disgrace of having me taking a whuppin' whenever another gang caught me alone.

Beginning in the early 1960s, karate was becoming popular, mainly because of its portrayal on the television shows *I Spy, The Detectives, The Avengers,* and *The Wild, Wild West.* Having decided that learning karate would turn me into a killing machine, I located a gentleman who taught the art on weekends in his backyard. During the next two Saturdays, which amounted to about three hours of instruction, I learned a few basic moves and two techniques against a push and a lapel grab. At the end of my second lesson, I was told that I needed to start paying two dollars a lesson, which brought my training to a sudden halt.

It didn't matter because I was satisfied that in these two lessons I'd become the King of Karate and quit. The following day I hit the streets, convinced that I was a lethal killer and that everyone should fear me. I strutted around like this for a week until a burly white guy walked up to me and hit me with a solid right cross that sent me to the ground, half senseless. For a while I felt defeated and discouraged. Although I didn't like getting punched in the face, I did like the confidence I felt before getting punched. It was enough to cause me to renew my karate training.

About a month later I found a karate teacher named Donald Griffith, who was a student of Fumio Demura. "Griff" was a black man who taught a hard style of karate called Shotokan. In return for cleaning the school, I wasn't charged for my lessons. Unlike my previous class that was taught informally in the backyard to students dressed in T-shirts and Levis, the Shotokan school was strict and formal.

My main motivation for learning karate was to hurt white people. I'd had enough of their negatively impacting my life. I figured that once I became skilled at martial arts, no white man would ever again dictate how I was going to act and what I was going to think.

Most of all, never again was a white man going to throw me out of my own home, especially in the presence of my mother.

Eventually a gang accepted me as a member, and I began hanging with the brothers at the local Foster's Freeze and spending less time at school. Every day was the same. We hung around the pool hall, shot dice in the alley, roamed the streets, and then returned to our turf at the Freeze. Everywhere we went we caused trouble. Besides fighting, we snatched purses from white women, stole hubcaps, and shoplifted from the local stores. As time passed, I saw more and more gang members being sent off to juvenile hall and being put on probation. Several members over the age of 18 ended up doing jail time, which worried me.

As I began to feel the heat of law enforcement, I befriended a black policeman named Julius Fisher. He was the first reserve policeman in the city of Monrovia and the first cop I admired.

I'd be swaggering down the sidewalk, and he'd pull his police car to the curb, roll down the window, and motion me over. I'd always look around to make sure no one saw me talking to the police, which was never a good idea. Fisher kept telling me that I needed to find another direction in life, and he burned this into my consciousness. He was a proud black man who felt good in his own skin, and he kept telling me, "You're a black kid. You can make something of yourself. You don't have to be out here roaming the streets looking for trouble." He saw the writing on the wall and wanted to prevent me from ruining my life before it was too late. It wasn't that I was in trouble, but he knew that it wouldn't take long before I would be.

Although I honestly wanted to make something of myself and become successful, I never had any role models, and, in fact, I'd never known a successful black person in Savannah. There may have been some, but I never met them. And even if any did exist, they surely weren't coming to my impoverished neighborhood to mentor me.

Regardless, I was determined to get even with white people and to outdo all of them. Somehow, some way, I was going to turn the tables completely around and get white people answering to me. From everything I'd observed in life and on television, the way I planned to do this was by becoming a millionaire. Money was the key to getting white people to listen for my giddy-up, instead of the other way around.

As I entered my senior year of high school my classmates were making plans for college or entering the workplace. In sharp contrast, I was now looked upon as the town joke, a screw up with no future. Throughout the previous two years the girls thought I was funny and cool, but now they all but ignored me. No one had to tell me to my face that I was a loser because it was obvious.

I was angry with my biological father, with James Vaughn, and especially with God. In my mind, with the exception of my mother, for the past 17 years all the people who should have helped me only added grief to my life. Although my momma continued to take me to church, it did nothing to curb my anger. To me, God was just another entity that wanted to exercise control over my life.

My mother insisted that I was to be in church for the entire Sunday—Sunday morning, Sunday school, Sunday service, and Sunday night service. Throughout the rest of the week, whenever she could corner me at home, she'd read to me from the Bible. After a lifetime of this, I began to hate that book. Whenever I did something wrong, she'd set me down and lecture me. "You know what the Lord said, boy? I can't be-LIEVE you talked back to your teacher that way. Do you know what the Word of God says about that, boy?" Because of my momma's persistence, I was always bothered whenever I did wrong, and I felt this way from as far back as my childhood in Savannah.

Although I never dared question my mother, whenever she'd haul out the Bible and preach to me about how God provides, I wanted to say to her, "It sounds real good in theory, Momma, but I'm looking at you struggling throughout your whole life, oppressed in the Deep South, unable to get a good job, abandoned by my father to raise four kids on your own, losing our house to a fire in Savannah, and having that thieving white preacher Vaughn take off in the middle of the night and leave us flat broke. I mean, it doesn't sound to me like God's been providing."

But whenever I saw the peaceful look in her eyes and witness her living faith and abundant gratitude, I knew that we saw the world from entirely different perspectives. Because of this, I already knew what her answer would be. She'd light up with God in her eyes and say, "But, son, through all of that, look what God has done–you're not hungry, we have a roof over our head, I got a job, you got clothes. Through all that we went through, child, can't you see God? I didn't have a husband, but I raised you and you never missed a meal. Can't you see God in the fact that you, as a child, were sick, and look at you now in good health. What else do you want God to do?"

As I continued to run with the gang, the level of violence gradually escalated. What began as common everyday fighting in the street or the local park soon turned to felony assault. One day at the pool hall one of the gang members hit a guy in the head with a pool stick, and then grabbed his wallet and walked out the door. Besides assault, that was armed robbery. Although I was becoming scared about where the increasing violence was leading, I found that I had to continually prove myself in order to stay in favor with the gang.

Not long after the pool hall incident, I faced a major turning point in my life. One day while standing outside the Freeze, a white man pulled his car to a stop at the intersection, and on a dare from one of the gang members I took a four-foot length of heavy steel chain, walked behind the car, and violently threw it through his back window. I mean, that window didn't just crack. It exploded. And the sound was deafening. I literally stood there in shock, looking through the shattered rear window at the driver, who had a look on his face of sheer terror.

For as long as I live I'll never forget the look on that man's face. Later that evening when I was alone in my bedroom, I thought about the possibility of my actions having resulted in the man's having a heart attack or being killed or permanently crippled because out of fear he gunned his car through the red light and created a serious accident. I'd never done something that violent, and I was worried about what the gang might "dare" me to do next. Would it ultimately be necessary for me to kill someone in order to prove myself? I had to stop.

My momma always told me that I could accomplish anything I put my mind to as long as I believed in myself. She also often said that the two most important goals were for her children to get an education and to serve God, and I'd done neither. My brother had graduated from high school, and my sister was married and had a child, so in everyone's eyes they were successful. To the contrary, I was destined to live on the streets on welfare. I was going to be the only one who didn't make something of his life. I'd turn out no better than those hoboes back in Savannah. More than letting myself down, it hurt that I was letting my mother down, although she never mentioned it.

Shortly after I turned 17, I saw a photograph of my father. My momma had kept it for years in a cinder box and decided to show it to me. It was a tiny black-and-white photo that had fold marks, scratches, and in one place was torn. I was overwhelmed with emotion as I looked down at this tiny thumbnail photo of my father that had been taken a month before I was born. Dressed in overalls, he resembled a typical uneducated oppressed slave from the Jim Crow South. His skin was a lot darker than I'd envisioned, and his expression was that of a man who had worked hard, but was constantly destroyed by the prejudice he encountered in Southern society.

I stayed up most of the night looking at that photo, trying to get a sense of what he might be trying to convey to me. Just before sunrise, the words that suddenly came to me were of a father saying, "I love you, son." As I fell off to sleep, holding the photo close to my heart, I promised my father that I wouldn't let him down the way he'd let me down, and that I hoped that one day I could find it in my heart to forgive him.

Faced with failing out of school, going to prison, or ending up in an early grave, I considered joining the military. I recalled my childhood years in Savannah watching movies on TV that depicted the WWII and the Korean War eras. These films featured great leading men like John Wayne, Montgomery Cliff, Robert Mitchum, Burt Lancaster, and Clark Gable. They were all dressed in neatly pressed military uniforms and rugged battle gear. I liked the idea of the military making a man of me and my returning to California as an officer and a gentleman. While I worked on polishing my new image, the women who fought over me could busy themselves polishing my medals.

The only military recruiter in my part of town was a naval recruiter, which sounded good to me, considering my childhood background in Savannah of building rafts and floating around the flood zone with my brother Marion. Perhaps over time and with the proper training, the Navy would make me captain of my own ship.

Days later I arrived at the naval recruiting office and took a seat in the small waiting area. There were posters on the walls that showed happy young sailors dressed in Navy blues and enjoying the good life in a variety of attractive settings.

After filling out a half-dozen forms, I sat at the desk of the recruiter, who told me I'd come to the right place. The Navy was prepared and eager to offer me the four best years of my life— and much more if I decided to make a career of the Navy, which according to the recruiter wouldn't surprise him in the least. In addition to becoming eligible for the GI bill and a ton of other benefits, I'd be spending a leisure life traveling the world on the open seas. What an opportunity. Good food, my own private quarters, shuffleboard on the main deck, and shore leave at some of the most exciting cities in the world. I imagined sipping an expensive glass of wine in a Parisian café as beautiful French women seated at neighboring tables admired me, the man wearing the proud uniform of the United States Navy.

I had only one concern. The year was 1965, and the Vietnam crisis was heating up. The recruiter smiled confidently. There was no need to worry. The problem in Vietnam was being handled by ground troops and should be over in a few months. Besides, I'd be far away on a big naval ship that typically were surrounded by a fleet of other ships and were further protected by submarines lurking beneath the water.

I could taste the ocean air as he wrapped up his pitch. I had only one question as I relaxed back in my chair and smiled, "How do I sign up?"

chapter seven

Military

Two weeks after enlisting in the Navy, I arrived at San Diego's Naval Training Center (NTC). When I stepped off the bus, I was lined up with 50 other raw recruits and addressed by a black drill sergeant, who greeted us with a friendly smile. "How are you girls?

At first I thought I hadn't heard right. I looked around at the others who were as dumbfounded as I was. The sergeant continued with his warm greeting. "One thing I want to share with you girls is that I'm going to be your momma for the next six months. I *may* be your daddy, but I'm *definitely* going to be your momma because I'm going to hug you and love you just like your momma does. Now if any of you have a problem with that, please let me know now so that we can work it out."

I was flabbergasted. What kind of welcome was that? We were supposed to be military men. I stood frozen like everyone else, as he continued. "You see that line over there? That yellow line? I want you all to go line up on that yellow line side-by-side. I'll be back." And with that, he returned to his nearby office and disappeared inside.

Moments later we were handed our military issue and told to set it neatly on the ground. My first two orders had gone well—stand on the yellow line and, two, make a nice pile out of my newly-acquired uniforms and toiletries. Maybe this was going to work out all right. Six months of push-ups and run around a little bit, a couple days of shooting practice, play cards and shoot dice on my days off. The food wasn't as good as my momma's, but I'd live with it for six months until I headed out for the open seas in style. And that drill sergeant—I guessed he was all right—was a kidder, like me. Maybe we'd become best friends by the time this little shindig was over.

My reverie was abruptly shattered as the door to the sergeant's office flew open and crashed against the side of the building. The sergeant stormed over to us and, with a murderous look in his eyes and breathing fire, singled me out.

"I told you to line up, Mistah! What is your problem!"

I feared he was going to pull my head off and was relieved when he turned away and began his real indoctrination speech, which lasted ten minutes. By the time he finished, he'd succeeded in making it abundantly clear that he was going to be the boss of me for the next six months, and that if I had any problem with that, he definitely was going to pull my head off.

The military taught me the true meaning of respect. When I was a child growing up in Georgia, white people didn't have to earn my respect, nor did I have to earn theirs. I simply showed them respect because I was told to. When I came to California, I learned that respect had to be earned. The way you earned respect in the street was either through whuppin' someone or having everyone agree that you could. You earned respect by proving yourself to others.

At boot camp in San Diego, that black drill instructor had earned the stripes he wore on his sleeve long before I arrived. They were given to him by men who knew a whole lot more about the military and about combat than I did. The military taught me to salute all men who wore stripes, clusters, bars, and medals on their uniforms. These men didn't have to earn my respect. Someone else awarded them rank, and it wasn't me.

The military also taught me to follow orders and to do so without trying to find a way around them or questioning why. From day one, the military had no intention of putting up with my clowning or excuse making. For a comedian, the military was a tough room. And I did try, although my efforts were short-lived. The age-old excuse that the dog ate my homework fell on deaf ears. By the end of my first two weeks, I'd had my fill of running ten miles around the grinder, which was an asphalt parking area the size of a football field, with 80 pounds of full battle gear strapped to my back.

I figured out in record time that as far as the military was concerned, I could spend my entire six months in boot camp running around the grinder, cleaning latrines, and doing pushups—and if I really pushed my luck they'd have me washing a battleship with a Q-tip. So I learned to follow orders. Becoming a team player instilled in me a sense of security because I realized that everyone else was also following orders and that on the battlefield human life depended on it.

After six months, I graduated boot camp. I was top in my group and honored to be asked to carry the flag on the day of the ceremony. For the first time in my life, I had finished something I'd started. When I attended junior high and high school, I didn't have the ability to complete the work that my teachers had assigned because I hadn't received an adequate preparatory education in Georgia. But the military treated me fairly. My superiors never gave me an assignment without also providing me with the training I needed to carry out their orders. When I graduated, I felt a degree of pride and for a short while thereafter, my anger and hostility toward white people subsided.

Two days after graduating boot camp, I was shipped out to an Air Force base in Kingsville, Texas. When I arrived, the military had no immediate place to assign me, so I was classified as a general seaman with no specialty. After a few weeks, my superiors finally figured out how a recruit who had been the honored flag bearer at his graduation from boot camp could best serve his country, and I was ordered to report to the kitchen where I ultimately ended up peeling potatoes.

I'd never in my life seen so many potatoes. I didn't spend an hour peeling 100 potatoes for the officer's potato salad or for a scalloped potato dish for the evening meal. I peeled hundreds and hundreds of potatoes every day for an entire shift. I had become that clueless comic book character Sad Sack, whom I remembered from my childhood. The more potatoes I peeled, the more arrived. I felt like the Sorcerer's apprentice with two buckets fighting an endless flood of water, only I was flooded with an endless pile of potatoes.

This was it? For the next three years I was going to be peeling potatoes in Kingsville, Texas? By the second week it dawned on me that everyone working in the kitchen was black, except for our supervisor, who was white. I felt used and that I'd been had. If I could have gotten my hands on that naval recruiter in Rocktown, I would have wrung his neck the way my momma had wrung the necks of our chickens in Liberty City.

In an attempt to relieve my frustration, I decided to renew my karate training. I had a solid background in karate, and the military had put muscle on me. I stood well over six feet tall and weighed 190 pounds. More importantly, I now had a sense of commitment and discipline.

I scoured the local yellow pages and located a karate school that was close to the base. Two nights later I drove to the school and watched a class. The students were a sorry bunch of white guys. Brown belts doing basic two-step block movements— nothing advanced, just punch and block while waltzing atop the mats, with an occasional lackluster kick thrown in just to break the monotony.

After the class ended, the head instructor walked over to me and asked what I wanted. When I told him I was interested in joining the school, he seemed anything but eager. Later I heard off the grapevine that the only reason I was allowed to join the school was because the rent was overdue. There was a catch, however. Because I was black, I was required to pay higher monthly dues.

The first night that I arrived for class dressed in my new karate uniform, the real guys showed up. I had no idea what had become of those bozos I observed earlier, but they were nowhere in sight. Upon spotting me, one of the black belts said, "Hey, here's some fresh meat," then added without the slightest hint of shame or disrespect, "Is this nigger going to train with us?" Except me, everyone laughed, and then proceeded to share what sounded like normal conversation. The initial racial remark didn't come off as racist, and the man who uttered it was so comfortable saying it that I didn't get mad. Not then, anyway.

My first month of training was pure hell. I'd arrive for class and the students wouldn't work out with me. I was just there. I guess they thought I'd quit, but I kept coming back, and I kept watching the black belts, and then I'd return to the base and practice on my own. Eventually I got good and the black belts got around to whuppin' on me. I became their toy. Like a dog gnaws on its favorite bone, these black belts gnawed on me.

Unfortunately for them, they didn't know what they were doing because if they had, they wouldn't have done it. Over the course of several months, they literally whupped me into perfection. By the time I left the school I'd whupped every white man in the place, which I'd vowed to do. And that guy who called me a nigger? He was my number one target. He must have heard the train bearing down on his stalled car on the tracks because he wisely quit before I could get to him. He knew I would have beaten him like a rug on a clothesline.

Back at the base my Sad Sack routine hadn't improved one bit, and I finally went to my commanding officer and pleaded my case. It wasn't that I wanted out of the military. I just wanted out of the kitchen. My commanding officer understood. He wanted the military to be a pleasant experience for me. When he was finished talking, he walked me into his outer office where a subordinate provided me with a dozen forms that could result in a more suitable assignment.

On the form that listed job priorities, I listed medic as my first choice. I figured that being a medic on a naval ship was good duty. Sailors would come to rely on me for dispensing aspirin for headaches and an occasional vial of seasickness pills. I'd probably end up dining with the officers. My second choice was to be trained as a barber. In a way I'd have my own office, and because I like to entertain people, well, nothing beats a barbershop.

The following week I was informed that I was going to be sent to Twenty-Nine Palms for training to become a medic. Glory be to God. I was out of the kitchen and one step away from enjoying the leisure life promised to me by that naval recruiter.

The training at Twenty-Nine Palms went relatively smoothly. For the most part I read manuals, worked on rubber mannequins, injected water-filled syringes into oranges and apples, and practiced suturing cuts of beef. I was finally back on course. As I fell asleep, I could smell the ocean air and hear the waves gently slapping the hull of my awaiting ship. Upon completing six weeks of training, I received my orders. I was assigned to the 3rd Marine Attachment and was being sent to the battlefields of Vietnam.

The "White Elephant" was so named by the Vietnamese because it was an enormous three-story white building. To the military, it was a field hospital located several miles from the war zone. Upon my arrival in Vietnam, I reported to the White Elephant where I spent the duration of my military service tending to the sick and wounded.

The daily routine was similar to what was depicted in the TV series "Mash." I spent most of my shift changing dressings, giving shots, and removing shrapnel from injured soldiers. When things were slow, I changed bedpans and catheters. The White Elephant was far enough from the battlefields that I felt safe.

Although technically I was a corpsman, no one called me that. Instead, like all medics, I was addressed as "Doc." I had a title, a red cross affixed to my arm, and a loaded .45 strapped to my waist. Medics had priority. When I went into the mess hall, I didn't have to stand in line like most everyone else. I was ushered through like an officer. To a degree my anger subsided again. It wasn't that I suddenly liked white people, but I tolerated them. This tolerance, however, was to be short-lived.

Not long after I arrived in Vietnam, my mother began writing, and we talked on the phone whenever I could afford it. Although she was proud of me, she was worried that I might be killed before "getting right" with the Lord. To her, this meant accepting Jesus as Lord and Savior and being baptized in Jesus' name, which I hadn't done.

Throughout my childhood years of my momma dragging me to church every Sunday, I never heard the name Jesus. I'm sure Jesus was mentioned dozens of times in every service, but I never heard it.

So this worried my momma and, without fail, in every letter and telephone conversation she'd bring that up. Moreover, she'd ask if I was going to church, praying, and reading my Bible daily. We wouldn't be two minutes into our conversation and she would ask, "Boy, are you serving the Lord?"

"Yes, Momma. You would've loved last Sunday's guest preacher. Oh, Momma, he was good!" The truth was I hadn't attended a single service. It bothered me to lie to her, but I didn't want her to worry.

As was often the case when I lied to my momma, I should have kept my mouth shut. Satisfied I was going to church, she'd break into her speech about tithing. To her, tithing was more important than paying the rent. "Your salary. Do you still get your military money?"

"Yes, Momma."

"Are you paying your tithe?"

"Momma, we don't have an actual church here. There's no building. We just meet and listen to preachers who are passing through."

"But, son, you're not giving God His?"

I just couldn't make her understand that we didn't have a church adjacent to the battlefields of Vietnam. And I knew enough about churches to know that you pay tithe at a place you call your church.

"Momma, I'll keep records and pay when I come home."

"No, son. You need to pay your tithe. Give it to that preacher."

"Yes, Momma," I said with a sigh of resignation, even though I had no idea where that guest preacher had gone.

I hadn't forgotten about the martial arts training that I started in Rocktown and then continued in Kingsville. In fact, I was more driven than ever. Shortly after arriving in Vietnam I joined a group of martial artists who were training regularly behind the barracks. We called our crude form of training "jailhouse karate" and worked out at sunrise or early evening to avoid the unrelenting heat and humidity.

Although collectively we came from a mixture of styles and levels of skill, our group was often led by a Korean named Mr. Yu, who had undergone years of formal training in Korea and held the rank of black belt. He demanded respect and would beat the daylights out of anyone who failed to bow to him or address him as Mr. Yu. This man was utterly phenomenal. From a standing position he could jump six feet off the ground and spin kick his opponent in the face, and follow up with several more blows on his way down.

For months I attended every workout taught by Mr. Yu. As my discharge date approached, I vowed to look him up once I returned to the States, that is, provided we both got out of Vietnam alive.

During my leisure time I often went downtown with other medics to shoot pool in the local bars and hang with the brothers.

Although I worked close to the war zone, I only heard about the battlefields. I wasn't in the trenches, although I did see firsthand the results of battle on the wounded and dying soldiers who were brought to the White Elephant.

One afternoon a convoy stopped by the local bar and its leader asked for volunteers to accompany the convoy on a local scouting mission. Because I'd volunteered for these sorts of missions before, I agreed to go along.

We weren't a half mile down the road when we were ambushed. Within seconds, bullets whizzed past my head, and several ricocheted off my helmet. There was no question in anyone's mind that we were in the middle of a kill zone. The barrage of crossfire was unrelenting. This was the first time I actually saw soldiers getting shot at with live fire. In my six weeks training to be a medic, the military hadn't prepared me for this.

The driver gunned the transport vehicle toward a small hillside where there appeared to be American soldiers returning fire. When the truck stalled and its engine died, I leapt to the ground and took off running for cover. With bullets screaming past my head and kicking up the dirt at my feet, I was suddenly, and forcefully, pulled into a trench by a black infantryman. In the ten minutes that followed, someone got on the horn and called in for air support and most of us managed to avoid a date with death.

After the smoke cleared, the soldier who had yanked me into the trench looked at me and said, "Hey, aren't you Lissie's boy?" I just stared back at him. To this day, I have no idea who that man was or how he knew my mother. It occurred to me later that God must have been looking out for me that day. Thousands of miles away from the battlefield, my momma must have been praying really hard.

In the weeks following the ambush, I reflected on those ten minutes I spent in that trench under live fire and my racial anger soared to a new high. Along with the men who arrived in that convoy, the men in that trench were black. Then I got to thinking about the wounded and dying who were brought to the White Elephant, and it occurred to me that the great majority were poorly educated blacks who had taken direct orders from white officers.

The best a black man could do in the military was to attain the rank of sergeant, which was a non-commissioned officer. Today in retrospect I know there were white soldiers fighting in Vietnam, but at the time I didn't see them. Again I began to feel like a second class citizen and viewed the way I'd been treated by the military as a gross injustice, and I took it personally.

I stewed for weeks. My anger and hatred of white people boiled inside me like a pressure cooker whose valve finally blew one evening when I smarted off to five Marines who were leaving a bar where they'd been drinking. We exchanged words, and I honestly thought I could whup them all, and told them so. Three were skinny, but it didn't matter. One by one, they beat the living daylights out of me. Although I'd trained in karate for six months, these guys were hardcore Marines who knew how to inflict a real ass whuppin'. They weren't trying to kill me. They just wanted to whup my behind and let me know who was in charge. I put up a good fight, and to this day feel I earned their respect, even though I lost. When it was over, I lay on the ground with chipped teeth, cut knees, and shoulders that felt like they were out of joint.

During my week of hospitalization, all I thought about was getting out of that bed so that I could get tougher and get even. Payback time was coming. I had a serious score to settle with white people—and I meant business.

chapter eight

Becoming Empowered

When I was discharged from the military, I remained passionate about the martial arts and sought out Mr. Yu, who had since opened a karate school in Northern California in the small community of Hayward.

Mr. Yu remembered me from our training sessions behind the barracks and offered me a position managing the school in return for my karate lessons. In addition, he allowed me to sleep at the school at night. I became what was known as "dojo janitor." I continued training with Mr. Yu and managing his school, and after two years was awarded a black belt in the Korean martial art of Tae Kwon Do.

During my idle time, I read martial arts magazines and came across several articles about a black man named Steve Sanders, who was making a name for himself in karate tournaments. Steve was a former Marine who served in Vietnam and was also around my age. In six months he'd placed in several tournaments and was one of only a handful of black competitors. In the several brief articles that I read about him, little was mentioned about his personal life other than the fact that he lived in Southern California.

In the late 1960s, many of the top martial arts organizations were based in Los Angeles, as was the biggest karate tournament in the world, held each year in Long Beach. Convinced that my martial arts career was stalling in the remote town of Hayward and determined to make a name for myself in the karate world, I thanked Mr. Yu for all his help and headed south.

During the time I was stationed in Vietnam, my mother moved from Rocktown to the neighboring town of Monrovia. Although the rocks were gone, Monrovia wasn't unlike most black ghettos.

My momma was happy to see me and began hanging my clothes in the spare bedroom only minutes after I arrived. That evening I sat with her at the kitchen table eating fried chicken, yams, collard greens, and corn muffins. Momma hadn't changed one bit.

"Oh, Momma, you don't even know how good this is."

"Praise the Lord. He's the one who provides."

I glanced at the ancient washboard that stuck out of a number two metal tub. "I wish He'd provide you with a new washing machine instead of that old washboard you're still using."

"Washboard do just as good as them newfangled machines."

"Those lily white machines aren't made for us poor black folk."

"Son, why you always want to talk so racial? You know what the Bible says about that."

"Just telling it like it is, Momma."

"I don't care. It's ungodly."

We talked into the evening. She wanted me to look into my GI bill benefits and return to school, but I had other plans. As far as I was concerned, I didn't need to learn a trade or spend four years in college earning a degree. I already had a degree. I had a black belt.

My mother knew next to nothing about karate, except what she'd read in my letters. To her, karate was some strange Japanese sport where grown men dressed in funny looking pajamas kick and yell at each other and break boards. She had absolutely no understanding of how anyone, especially a black man, could make a living teaching karate.

I spent the next hour telling her about Steve Sanders, who many felt was as good as Bruce Lee, and how there were karate tournaments springing up everywhere and that martial arts was starting to be featured on television and in the movies. She smiled quietly and nodded occasionally, but as far as she was concerned the whole thing sounded foolish. She kissed me on the cheek and told me she'd wake me early the next morning for church.

During the next week I drove around Los Angeles trying to hook up with a karate school and got nowhere. It wasn't a matter of my being black, although I felt that had something to do with it.

The problem, so I was told, was that I wasn't trained in the school's system and by its master. And these schools were all cliquish. The basic styles were Japanese, Chinese, and Korean, many of which had offshoots, and none of which recognized the others. Worst of all, none of these masters were willing to honor my black belt and wanted me to start over again as a beginning white belt.

After several days of this, I got so fed up that I became belligerent and physically challenged several masters to step onto the mats with me—and in their schools.

The other major source of frustration was that no one seemed to know where I could find Steve Sanders. While a few thought they'd heard the name somewhere, no one knew where he trained.

I spent two days checking out the few remaining schools on the list I'd compiled from the yellow pages and came to one major conclusion. I had to make a name for myself by showing these people what I could do. This business of sitting across the desk from someone trying to sell myself hadn't worked. I needed to bust somebody's head in order to make a statement.

As I was driving back to my mother's house, I spotted a young black man entering a boarded up movie theater, a rolled up karate uniform bound with a black belt slung over his shoulder. I eyed him for a long while in the rearview mirror and made an illegal U-turn.

The old theater was dimly lit. I entered and observed six black martial artists working out, while two sparred on the bare stage. The taller of the two stood motionless in a stance, and then countered his opponent's attack with a solid kick.

"Damn, Karl, you gonna knock the wax outta his ears!" one of the observers yelled.

The man who was kicked playfully objected. "Say what? The monkey ass never touched me!"

They laughed as the taller man danced around, holding his hands victoriously overhead. Moments later he walked over to me. "What's happening, bro?" he said in a friendly manner.

I eyed him testily. "I was about to ask you that."

"Excuse me?"

"You call that fighting? Looks more like they're playing pattycake."

The man's smile disappeared. "I take it you study the art."

"I *teach* the art."

"Right on. Care to join in?"

"No question I could teach you guys a whole lot, only I'm not feeling charitable today," I replied, determined they were going to honor my black belt one way or the other.

"Charitable?"

"That's what I said." Then I added loudly and deliberately, "From what I've seen, I can whup any black belt in the place."

Several heard the remark and paused in their training.

The man glared back evenly. "What was that?"

"You heard me." And even louder, "I said I can whup any black belt in the place!"

Everyone eyed me, and then slowly turned their collective gaze to a dark corner of the stage.

"Really? the man said with a wry grin. "Well … can you whup Steve Sanders?"

I stiffened, disbelieving what I thought I just heard. "Sanders?"

"Yeah. Steve Sanders."

I followed their gaze and spotted a lean, muscular black man glaring back at me from the shadows. There was no doubt in my mind that I was looking at Steve Sanders because I'd seen pictures of him in karate magazines. He appeared to be anything but amused. I swallowed hard, then replied with all the bravado I could muster up, "Me and Steve Sanders can whup all of ya'!"

The tension hung in the air, and then Sanders broke out laughing and was quickly joined by the others.

Steve Sanders (he subsequently had his name legally changed to Steve Muhammad) lived in South Central Los Angeles in a small house that had a rickety porch, torn screens, and was in need of paint. The interior was as drab as the outside. The furniture was secondhand and there was no flair for decor, just utility. His place was typical of what I'd seen in the other black ghettos.

From the first day we met, Steve and I hit it off, and it wasn't long before I left my momma's and moved into Steve's spare bedroom. The room was small and dingy, and my bed was an old mattress thrown on the floor.

While Steve worked days at the Hostess Bakery, where he had been employed for two years, I trained in his basement and taught private karate lessons on the side. I didn't make much money, but it was enough to help keep Captain Crunch cereal in the pantry and milk in the fridge. Sometimes money was so tight that I lived on day-old bread and Hostess Twinkies that Steve brought home from work.

Over the next year Steve and I became closer and met each other's family. Whenever Steve trained in the martial arts, I was there. He didn't teach me as a student as much as I learned from just being around him.

Steve was the first black man who had something I wanted. As a martial artist he was in a league by himself. He could whup people by accident, while I whupped them on purpose. Moreover, he was well-mannered, college educated, and profoundly confident.

I wanted to be just like him, not only as a martial artist, but as a man. Unlike me, he'd grown up in a middle-class family in Kansas where he starred on the college football team and was so good that he was offered a professional football career.

I began going with Steve to compete in tournaments, which had grown considerably and become more competitive since I'd moved in with Steve a year earlier. Everything about these tournaments was bigger—the number of competitors, the entry fees, and the prize money. Most of all, the notoriety gained by a grand champion could result in television and film appearances.

Unfortunately for us, as well as the handful of other black martial arts competitors, tournament competition was dominated almost exclusively by whites and Asians who were backed by well-established organizations. As a result, biased judging was common, as well as how some promoters structured the elimination rounds. Black fighters were often pitted against each other in order to cut the field of blacks, and it was not unusual for a black fighter to fight more matches than those fought by whites and Asians.

The biggest problem Steve and I encountered was that we weren't backed by a prominent martial arts organization. In fact, we weren't even part of a school. We just walked into tournaments and signed up.

None of this bothered Steve. He just fought longer and harder. I, however, had an entirely different reaction. My anger soared whenever judges ignored the footprint I left on my opponent's gi jacket after I'd scored a solid kick. On more than one occasion I was disqualified for heatedly arguing with the officials. And there were several times that Steve physically removed me from the arena before I took a swing at some honky.

After six months of enduring what I perceived as a gross injustice, Steve and I, along with a group of other black martial artists, formed the Black Karate Federation (BKF). We leased a boarded up commercial building that had been burned in the Watts riots and hung out our shingle. Along with scores of previously unaffiliated black martial artists who joined our organization, we recruited tough street blacks from South Central and taught them how to convert their highly effective street fighting ability into karate. And when we felt that we finally had a kick-ass fighting team, we headed back to the tournament circuit.

Members of the BKF didn't meander into tournaments—we *marched* onto the main floor carrying black briefcases and wearing leather trench coats, sporting Afros, and singing our school's fight song. The martial arts community wasn't prepared for this, but there really wasn't anything they could do about it. We were more than show. We began winning, and winning big.

Having publicly gained the reputation of a racist, I made no bones about targeting white martial artists, and I relished in the psychological edge I had over white competitors who, thanks to the media, connected the BKF with the Black Panther Party, Muhammad Ali, and the highly feared black street gangs of the inner cities. Whether truth or fiction, I never missed an opportunity to feed the egregious legend, and I made a point of empowering my BKF comrades with words and slogans depicting black power.

For the first time in my life I felt that I'd gained an upper hand over white people through my ability to instill fear in them. I was backed by Steve Sanders, who was the toughest black martial artist in the country, and by the most feared karate organization in the world, the BKF.

Muhammad Ali was my hero, and I soon began modeling my behavior after him. I was a brazen, loud, often humorously clever black fighter who taunted and ridiculed my opponents at every opportunity. It wasn't long before I was given the name "The

Clown Prince of Karate." I'd park my '54 Cadillac limousine, which was completely restored, in front of the Long Beach Sports Arena, and when the parking attendant would tell me I couldn't park there, my entourage would say, "That's Donnie Williams from the BKF. He can park wherever he wants."

Moreover, I was an early version of Dennis Rodman. I wore flashy clothes accented with outrageous capes and designer sunglasses, and I wouldn't allow anyone, especially white people, to address me by anything other than Mr. Williams.

My gig paid off, and over a year's time I won the California State Tournament, Texas Championship, both the West Coast and East Coast Karate Championships, the Pan American, and the Four Seasons tournaments. I didn't win these tournaments because I was a great martial artist. I won because I had a burning obsession to beat white people. Before each championship match, I'd go off quietly somewhere and tap into my intense racial hatred, which I utilized to ignite my most primitive survival instinct. Moments later when I faced my opponent, my mind, body, and fighting spirit reacted as if I were facing someone who wanted to kill me. And it worked. My reflexes and speed doubled, my timing was dead on, my opponent appeared on my radar screen in slow motion, and my blows were delivered as if on autopilot. I rocketed to victory on the jet fuel of years of fierce racial hatred.

As a result of winning a string of major tournaments I was offered work in films. In 1972 I appeared in a scene for the movie *Enter the Dragon* starring Bruce Lee, which was followed by work on *Black Belt Jones* starring Jim Kelley, *Truck Turner* starring Isaac Hayes, and *Li Hsio Lung Chaun Chi* starring Bruce Li. In addition to bit parts and walk-ons, I helped choreograph the fight scenes for Clint Eastwood in *The Gauntlet*. In a strange way I felt that my notoriety might come to the attention of my father, wherever he was, and that maybe it would result in his getting in touch with me, but he never did.

To all outward appearances I'd finally become successful. I was hanging around a substantial list of rich people, including Hollywood celebrities and corporate magnets, riding in Rolls Royces and flying on private jets, wearing fancy clothes, and often strolling with a woman on each arm.

The problem was I didn't feel successful. I felt that rich white people saw through the veneer, and that to them I was nothing more than an uneducated, socially unpolished black karate fighter who didn't have two nickels to rub together. I'd go out with a beautiful woman and do my best to impress her and show her a night on the town with "the man," but when the evening ended and she suggested going back to my place, I felt like the Wizard behind the drape because I didn't have a mansion to take her to.

It was as if I were living two different lives. On the one hand I was a smooth talking, slick brother—a lying, sweet talking dude—who was working in movies and had this stellar reputation as a champion karate fighter, yet on the other hand I didn't own a car aside from my decades-old limo, which was really my gig and my flow show. I was bothered by the fact that white people could get away with being rich, although appearing to be poor. Howard Hughes was once the richest man in the country and he drove around in junk heaps and lived in squalor, but no one ever treated him as anything but highly successful because he was a multimillionaire. If a white man drove a Rolls Royce, everyone assumed it was his car, but if I were to drive that same Rolls, most people would assume that I was driving someone else's car or that I was the chauffeur taking the car to be washed. No matter what I did, I always ended up feeling that I was back in Liberty City, walking to church in those same ugly shoes.

Even my martial arts career didn't sit well with me. When I first met Steve Sanders years earlier, my ultimate goal was to become the world karate champion. And while I won a half-dozen major tournaments, I never won the Superbowl of karate—the

Long Beach Internationals, which was where Bruce Lee was first introduced to the martial arts world and great fighters like Chuck Norris, Mike Stone, and Billy Blanks earned their stripes and made their reputations. A fighter could win every tournament there was to win in the world, but if he didn't win the Long Beach Internationals, no one remembered him. It was like a football team winning its division but losing the Superbowl, or a baseball team winning the pennant but losing the World Series. Second place didn't count. The Long Beach Internationals was irrefutably the tournament of tournaments.

As much as I tried to convince myself that not winning the world title didn't matter, in my most quiet moments I knew that it did. And it wasn't that I hadn't come close. I had. There were several times when I spent all day fighting my way through the eliminations, but when it came to the championship match, I lost. And I was angry about that. I felt that I'd lost because I was black and was cheated. In 1976, I was approaching 30, and there was a wave of new, hungry young warriors coming onto the circuit. My confidence in my Muhammad Ali clown act was beginning to wane.

It was around this time that I received an offer to appear in a film that required me to spend three months in Japan. There wasn't much else going on in my life at the time, and I felt that getting away might be a good idea. Perhaps in my absence the stars would realign themselves in my favor, and when I returned things would be different. I was growing so despondent that one night I found myself saying a fleeting prayer that something major had to change in my life. Unbeknownst to me, I was about to be a prime example of the old adage "watch out what you pray for."

chapter nine

Valerie

The time spent in Japan was a godsend. I was a stranger in a strange land, but it felt good. Besides making some much needed money, no one in Japan cared that I was black. Best of all, the only whites I saw were tourists, and we were a long way from the Deep South, which suited me just fine.

For three months I worked with Japanese martial arts star Tadashi Yamashita on the filming of *Za Karate III*, and then flew back to California. The day following my return, I renewed my hip, slick, and cool California image, donning my knit cap, shiny silk shirt, bright red pants, designer sunglasses, and patent leather shoes.

After the film project in Japan ended, I didn't have anything lined up and was struggling to keep things together. I was working at a recording studio helping to produce an album when a friend named Jay stopped by. During our conversation he mentioned that his girlfriend Judy wanted to introduce me to a friend of hers named Valerie Juarez. Being the consummate player, I agreed to turn on the charm and make this Valerie woman's day—and better yet her night if she turned out to be super fine. When Jay relayed my answer, Judy said that she and Valerie would stop by the studio sometime the following week.

Prior to meeting Valerie, I asked Jay to give me the lowdown on her. It wasn't that I was all that interested, just curious. According to Judy, Valerie was a relatively attractive Hispanic woman who had been previously married, lived in a small apartment with her young son Chuck, and worked at a toy factory inspecting toys on an assembly line. So far, she didn't qualify as marriage material, but I was still willing to consider her as a potential notch on my bedpost. Moreover, Valerie, who grew up in the barrio, had been raised Catholic, although none of her family attended church regularly. Having been raised in a traditional Mexican family, she was taught from an early age by her mother to be submissive, particularly to her father. I liked the sound of that. This woman wasn't going to give me trouble. Things were looking up.

A week later the girls came by the studio. Although I'd briefly spoken with Jay's girlfriend Judy on the phone, I'd never personally met her, and Jay never mentioned that she was a big fan of mine. Judy was no sooner in the door than she yelled, "Donnie Williams!" and then handed me a magazine with a picture of me on the cover, which she wanted me to autograph.

I scribbled my name on the front then and kissed her on the cheek, which resulted in her blushing and giggling like a star struck teenager. When I was then introduced to Valerie, she was staring at Judy with a look that said, "What is the matter with you, girl?"

Only I chose not to read it that way. I thought she felt left out, so I walked over to her and gave her the same kiss. Instead of reacting as Judy did, Valerie looked at me like she'd just been kissed by the Maytag repairman. I spent the next five minutes telling Valerie about my recent filming in Japan, as well as my other film appearances and my stellar career as a martial arts tournament fighter. She took it all in, smiling occasionally, and then left. My gut feeling was that the woman was playing hard to get—and wasn't that good at it either.

The following week, Jay told me what Judy relayed to him regarding Valerie's first impressions of me. I smiled confidently, convinced that Valerie was now mine for the taking. To begin with, Valerie didn't care about my movies or my karate and felt that I went out of my way trying to impress her and was full of myself. Furthermore, she wasn't in the least bit attracted to my looks and didn't care if she ever saw me again.

At first I thought Jay was pulling my leg, but soon realized he was dead serious. "Valerie said this to Judy?" I asked. "And she knew that Judy would tell you and that you would tell me?" Jay wasn't sure, and I didn't care. "I'm going to get her," I said. "She's playing me. I'll get her in bed by … who does she think she's dealing with? Get Judy to arrange for the four of us to have lunch."

I put considerable preparation into our second date. My Afro was primped to perfection, and I wore my best threads and most erotic, killer cologne.

During lunch I poured on the charm, which included my surefire lines and most flirtatious gestures. When I left, I considered calling Valerie later that afternoon to arrange for an evening tryst, but decided to let her fall asleep that night wishing I were lying beside her.

The following day word came back from Judy. Although Valerie had a better time with me at lunch than she did on our first meeting, she felt that I was overly confident about getting her into a "romantic setting," which were her exact words, and that just wasn't going to happen. As before, she didn't care if she ever saw me again.

I sailed into round three with a vengeance and began calling her regularly and sending flowers and candy. Three months later I was still sending flowers and calling her and spending time with her son, who eventually treated me as his hero. But every time I dropped by Valerie's apartment, she wasn't interested in hearing about my impressive list of accomplishments and my plans to become richer and more famous. All she wanted to talk about was her sister.

No matter what I did or said, I couldn't get this woman into the bedroom, which essentially took away my biggest trump card. Just as I'd learned years ago that I could control men with my martial arts prowess, I'd learned to control women through sex. Experience had taught me that once I got a woman in bed, I owned her. The fact that Valerie wouldn't permit this essentially resulted in my having no control over her.

Finally, after four months without having sex, I decided to throw in the towel. What began as an uncomfortable swan song turned into my sharing my true thoughts and motivations since we first met. I trusted her enough that I felt she'd keep everything to herself, and if nothing else she might remember me as something other than an insincere playboy and a cad.

For two hours I told Valerie how I really felt. I told her that I knew that I embellished my accomplishments and that the reason I'd done this from the start was that I felt that if I could get her romantically hooked on me that she wouldn't leave me if she ever found out that I wasn't the man I was portraying. I told her about my impoverished upbringing in Liberty City and how my family lived in a shack, that I wasn't well educated, and that my father had left before I was born and how desperately I missed him.

Over those two hours I literally told her the pure unadulterated truth about me, which included all my insecurities and fears. Most important of all, I shared with her that since childhood I'd felt that it was a curse to be black, and that because of this feeling, I always felt that I had to prove myself to everyone. With tears welling in my eyes, I told her that I never had a sense of dignity and that I had always wanted to feel proud to be black—the way Steve Sanders felt—but that I'd never been able to accomplish that, no matter how hard I tried.

When I was done, she wiped tears from both our eyes, and then leaned over and kissed me passionately for the first time. The following morning we awoke in each other's arms, totally committed to one another.

Valerie never mentioned the interracial aspect of our relationship. This didn't concern me because I knew that she'd grown up in the barrio around Mexicans and blacks. Now that we were a couple, she told me that she was uncomfortable about telling her parents, specifically her father, who had always been adamant that his children not marry outside their race. It wasn't so much that Albert Juarez was a racist, but rather that his strict policy was based on strong ethnic pride. I wasn't all that concerned.

Because Valerie was afraid to tell her father about being with a black man, she first told her mother, who broke the news to the family patriarch. Mr. Juarez's response was swift in coming. From that moment forward, he never wanted to see Valerie again, no one in the family was to mention her name in his house, and that the next time he would see her would be in her coffin.

I'd fallen in love with Valerie because she was the only other person besides my mother who had ever accepted and loved me unconditionally. Valerie was drawn to the real Donnie Williams, not the man I'd falsely projected to the rest of the world. She loved me enough to be disowned by her own father and banned from her family home. So I was committed to win her father back, which Valerie truly believed would never happen in this life.

Valerie and I soon moved in together, and a year later we married and she became pregnant. During the ensuing nine months, as her abdomen grew, so did my frustration. In my eyes I still hadn't achieved success. My film career had pretty much fizzled out, as well as my prominence on the karate tournament circuit. In order to pay bills, I'd taken a job with the security wing of Housing and Urban Development (HUD), which paid just enough to put food on the table and pay the rent on our modest two-bedroom apartment. Was this what my life had come down to? A security guard with HUD? Had the white power structure finally uncovered my ruse and put me in my preordained place?

Once again, I began to grow angry. That Valerie's father showed no sign of coming around added to my frustration. Was his decision to disown his daughter truly based on ethnic pride, or was this really about my being black? Whatever the answer was, I felt that my life had gone nowhere, and now I had a child on the way.

More painful than ever was the fact that with all my public notoriety—my movies, my face prominently displayed on the front covers of magazines, the scores of interviews—another year passed and my father had still failed to get in touch.

Two months before the annual Long Beach Karate Internationals were to take place, I felt driven to start working out because I'd agreed to participate as a judge. The thought of walking into the Long Beach Sports Arena—me, the renowned "Clown Prince"—50 pounds overweight and not being able to fit into my karate uniform depressed me. But when I tried resuming my standard workouts of years past, I quit after three days. And once again, the fact that I'd never won the championship reared its ugly head.

In July 1977 my wife gave birth to our son, who we named Steven Carlos Williams after Steve Sanders and Chuck Norris. I was present at our son's birth, which was one of the most beautiful experiences of my life.

Two days later, on the night before the start of the Internationals, I thought of ways I might get out of going and even wished I would be taken sick, but it was of no use. I'd only be fooling myself. And besides, who would miss me, anyway? I went to bed that night, dreading the next morning. I fell off to sleep thinking about how winning the championship in my prime might have felt.

The tuxedoed ring announcer stood in the middle of the elevated main arena and spoke into a microphone to the packed house, "Mr. Williams to the center ring! Mr. Williams to the center ring—please!"

Wearing a gi and in plain sight of the packed house, I stood all but five feet from the announcer. I recalled walking onto the staging minutes earlier and thought it odd that my entrance elicited no applause whatsoever.

"This is the final call for Mr. Donnie Williams!" the announcer continued impatiently. "You have one minute before disqualification!"

I stared at the announcer in disbelief. "I'm here! I'm right here!"

The announcer glanced apathetically at me. Although his mouth was moving, I couldn't decipher what he was saying, except that I was fighting in the red corner. I looked around the ring and noticed that all four judges and the referee were Caucasians, as was my opponent, who stood across the ring in the white corner, smiling back at me and offering a childlike wave. I didn't recognize my opponent, which also troubled me. The man had the stature of a child midget. I glanced down to the ringside seating, expecting to see my usual rank and file of Black Karate Federation supporters. Instead, the seats were filled with white people who glared back at me like a Ku Klux Klan lynch mob.

As the announcer began the customary explanation of the rules and method of point scoring, my opponent unexpectedly charged across the ring and laid into me like a freight train. I helplessly attempted to fend off the onslaught of kicks and punches, which were punctuated by my being kicked out of the ring and crashing into the ringside seats. As the spectators cheered at the sight of my opponent victoriously jumping around the ring, I scrambled back onto the staging, my gi in tatters.

"What the hell was all that about!" I screamed.

The referee breathed fire. "Mr. Williams, I am not going to tolerate that foul mouth of yours! I don't care—in fact, I don't give a rat's ass—about your stupid claim to being the Clown Prince!"

"You can kiss my ass!" I roared back. "The fight wasn't even officially started!"

I was suddenly blind-sided by a powerful slap to the side of my face. I spun around to find my mother standing beside me, veins protruding from her neck.

"Momma, what are you doing here?" I gasped, having no idea how she had gotten into the ring.

"That man is your heavenly brother!" she said, pointing to my opponent.

"Heavenly what? Momma, this is a karate tournament! We're competing for–"

"You didn't come here to compete! You came here to humiliate this man with all your anger and racial hatred! Do you know what the Bible says about this!"

The crowd suddenly weighed in with jeering catcalls and guffaws. "Williams brought his momma!" "Sissy!" "Pantywaist!" "Where's your Superman cape, Willie Boy!"

The image of my mother instantly vanished, leaving me dumbstruck. Following what seemed like a time warp, my opponent charged me again. Only this time I fought in earnest, landing kicks and punches to his head and body.

Believing that I'd totally overwhelmed him, I looked at the judges, expecting to see their red flags held in the air. But they stared back at me with apathy.

Suddenly my opponent charged forward like a blitzing NFL linesman. I thrust my front leg out in a powerful sidekick, hitting him dead center in the chest. I felt my foot literally break through the man's chest and become stuck on a splintered ribcage that felt like rows of shark's teeth. With both of us screaming in agony, I managed to yank my foot free. There was blood everywhere.

"Point!" all four judges yelled in unison and raised their white flags.

I was stunned at the sight of the judges signaling a point for my opponent, who now appeared unscathed as he jumped around the ring with his arms again raised victoriously overhead.

"What the hell's going on here!" I yelled and then glanced down at my right foot, expecting it to be seriously injured. But instead of a bloody, mangled foot, I saw an oversized clown's shoe. As the jeers from the crowd became louder and louder, I felt as if I'd suddenly stepped from my body and was now looking back at myself standing alone in the middle of the ring dressed as Clarabelle the Clown from the popular 1950s TV series "Howdy Doody."

As quickly as my mother had moments earlier disappeared, the ring referee reappeared as Buffalo Bob. He led the audience in singing the show's popular theme song, with a slight twist, "It's Howdy Doody Time, It's Howdy Doody Time, Let's give a rousing cheer, the fool Clown Prince is here!"

Hysterical, I began to tear apart Clarabelle's costume, throwing the wig, rubber nose, and flowery polka dot blouse into the unseen audience. "This is bullshit!"

I froze as the audience fell into stark silence and the house lights came up to reveal all 50,000 spectators to be my father, Joe Williams, dressed in his worn overalls.

"Papa!" I cried out with widening eyes.

The kaleidoscope of Joes, individually and collectively, departed the huge auditorium, turning their backs on me and offering nothing more than a pathetic wave. "You ain't no son of mine! You never could whup no honky! I was right leavin' you with your momma! You ain't no man, boy!"

"Papa! Wait! Please! This ain't really me!"

Out of nowhere came the voice of my wife Valerie, "Honey, it's all right. You're okay. Wake up."

Darkness fell upon the auditorium's center staging as I awoke in my bed, looking up at my wife. "What?" I muttered, disoriented.

Valerie wiped perspiration from my forehead. "You were dreaming. You just had a bad dream, that's all."

chapter ten

Seeking God's Help

An hour later I drove into the VIP parking of the Long Beach Sports Arena, which was adjacent to the Queen Mary, docked to the west. The sight of the mammoth ocean liner had for years triggered anger in me after I learned that not a single black man had ever traveled across the Atlantic in one of the several hundred staterooms. Instead, they had in large numbers been relegated to positions of porters, janitors, and workers who spent long hours of grueling servitude in the vessel's hellish engine rooms.

I walked to the entrance of the Sports Arena where several hundred spectators and competitors were making their way into the building. I felt invisible. Except for a handful of perfunctory greetings, gone were the crowds of autograph seekers and fans of years past.

Inside the 75,000 square foot arena the overall sight was as breathtaking as always. Hundreds of martial artists dressed in colorful karate and kung-fu uniforms were gearing up for the weekend of battle. I made my way to the gathering of BKF competitors and offered my best pep talk.

Later that morning the arena was alive with the kids competition. Having been dragged to the competition by fathers convinced they had sired the next Bruce Lee, many of the kids were nervous.

Dressed in street clothes, I acted as center judge of one of the two dozen fighting rings. I motioned two adolescent brown belts to the center of the ring and prepared to start the match.

A black kid was fighting out of the white corner; a white kid fought out of the red corner. Moments after I signaled for the fight to begin, the white kid buckled his opponent over with a roundhouse kick to the stomach. I immediately stopped the match and issued a warning for excessive contact. "Hey, don't be so hard. Ya'all just competing."

I signaled for the fight to resume. Within seconds the white kid floored his opponent with a reverse punch to the solar plexus, causing the black kid to break out crying. I stopped the match and deducted a point for excessive contact, then pulled the offender aside and dropped to one knee. "What's your name, son?"

"Billy—sir," the boy answered nervously.

"Look, Billy, this is sport karate. This isn't full contact or knockout karate. And if you hit too hard again, I'm going to have to disqualify you."

Billy's face bundled up. "Yes, sir."

When the fight was resumed for the second time, the white kid kicked his opponent squarely on the side of the head, knocking him half-senseless. Angered, I disqualified him and was immediately confronted by the boy's father, Dave Jaffe, who raced into the ring.

"What the hell's wrong with you, Williams!" the man began yelling. "You don't need to be judging! Nobody can score any points! You make it look like there's a bunch of girls in there!"

Jaffe was built like a bank vault. Besides being Billy's father, he was the boy's instructor and a highly reputable black belt tournament competitor. Incensed by the sight of this white man getting in my face, I glared back at him evenly. "Whoa, man, hold it. Read the rules. It says excessive contact, you lose points and can be disqualified."

"Excessive contact! Nobody got hit that hard!"

I pointed to the nearby black kid who was sobbing in his mother's arms. "Right. So how come the kid's crying?"

"Probably because he's one of your crybaby students would be my guess."

"What!" I roared, my nostrils flaring.

Florence Street School, remodeled.

The Family Church International today.

Lissie, 1945.

Momma, 1950 in Savannah.

The only photo of my father
Joe Williams (circa 1945).

Joe Williams, photo restored.

Rocktown, 1963.

Rocktown, shortly after my first karate lesson.

Seaman Apprentice Williams.

Graduating from boot camp, 1965.

Petty Officer Williams, Vietnam, 1967.

My older brothers Ernest (left), Marion (center),
and me, 1966.

Steve (Sanders) Muhammad, 1968.

Early tournament competition. Note the scarcity of black fighters.

Steve and me, 1971.

Black Karate Federation logo.

"The Clown Prince of Karate."

On the karate tournament circuit.

Wearing my unique "floppy hat," 1975.

My acting years 1973-1977.

Valerie's father Albert.

Valerie's mother Dolores.

My son Donnie, Jr.

Our sons Chaaz (left) and
Steven (right), 1991.

My stepson Charles.

My stepdaughter Gina.

Lissie and her three sons, Ernest (left),
Marion (center), and me.

Momma and my sister Joerene, 1968.

My wife and I with Chuck Norris.

With record producers Harold Borens and Isaac Hayes, 1974.

Building The Family Church International.

Valerie and I, 2005.

With screenwriter and author Tom Bleecker.

"You heard me!" Jaffe fired back with a sneer.

My heart quickened and I clenched my fists, suddenly consumed by a tidal wave of racial hatred. "Kiss mine, you punk ass chump!"

The ruckus drew the attention of a dozen black belts that physically got between us. Jaffe didn't let up.

"You're not fooling anyone, Williams! You couldn't whip my baby sister! You're nothing but a broken down has-been with a closet full of moth-eaten capes and dumb looking hats! That clown act of yours has gotten real thin—boy!"

I attempted to lunge at Jaffe, but was restrained. "Boy! Just who do you think you're talking to, honky! I'll whup you—your momma—your grandpappy—your daddy for havin' sex with your momma—and anyone else you can name!"

A nearby parent yelled out, "C'mon, fellas! There're kids here!"

"Honky?" Jaffe chided. "Oh, I forgot—you've got a thing about white people! Tough shit, Williams! Being black is your problem!"

"My problem? No—I'm your problem! Let's take this outside!"

Jaffe laughed. "I don't have time to humor you, Williams. I've got a tournament to win. If you can break away from your half-dozen groupies, drop by the black belt division and watch me fight. I'll show you what a real black belt looks like."

Moments later, Steve could barely keep up with me as I stormed across the main floor of the arena and waded into the area where the BFK fighters were gathered.

"Sammy, give me your gi pants!"

Sammy Pace had just finished competing in the black belt forms division. I could see that the rage in my eyes alarmed him, and he was confused by what he thought he'd heard.

"Excuse me?"

"I left my gi at home." My upper body was too big to fit into Sammy's gi top. I spun on Al "Hot Dog" Harvey, a heavyset black belt. "Hot Dog, let me borrow your gi top and find me a black belt!"

Makeshift uniform in hand, I ran across the arena and up a

flight of stairs, entering a men's room. Steve arrived and watched me furiously tearing off my clothes. "Man, you really need to think this through."

"Nothing to think about," I replied, as I kicked off my shoes and sent them sailing.

"Hey, I'm serious. It's been two years since you fought in a tournament."

I sucked in 30 pounds of flab as I yanked on the drawstring of Sammy's gi pants. "I don't care about winning any tournament! I just want to break a damn rib or something, and foot sweep that chump and see his head hit the ceiling! After I beat his ass, I'll bow out!"

"But there's nearly a hundred guys in that division," Steve said. "You may have to fight all day."

I gathered up my clothes and headed for the door. "No problem, man."

I returned to the area of the main arena where the black belt fighters were getting ready to begin the eliminations. Hovering over a long table, I quickly scanned two large charts, looking for Jaffe's name. Across the table, a young man dressed in street clothes glanced up at me. "Can I help you with something?"
I threw 40 bucks and a crumpled entry form on the table. "Yeah, I want in," I replied and continued scanning the charts.

"You mean in the black belt sparring?"

"You got it. Put me with that chump Jaffe."

"Excuse me?"

I found Jaffe's name and jabbed my finger at it. "Right there! Dave Jaffe! Put me up against him!"

The man glanced at the chart and shook his head. "Can't do it. That chart's already locked. I can get you in, but only at the bottom of this other chart. You're a little late."

I stared at the man coldly. "Name's Williams."

"I know who you are, sir, but I can't redo the charts."

"Say what?"

The man indicated the chart on which Jaffe was listed, "These guys are about to start the first eliminations."

I spun the chart around and quickly read the second round names just to the right of Jaffe. If Jaffe were to win, he would next fight the winner of the match between Ray Hudson and Paul Doucette. I knew that Hudson was a puny accountant who had never won a match in his life and probably never would. "What if I can get Doucette to switch with me in the first round?"

"But these guys are already set," the man answered sheepishly and offered a weak smile.

"Do you know who I am!" I screamed, looking like I was about to tear his head off.

Startled, the man jumped back. "Hey, all right. Relax. I'm sorry, okay?"

Scanning the crowd of black belt contestants, I spotted Doucette and was on him in seconds with my heated request. But Doucette wouldn't trade because he knew his first fight was with a little chump, and he wouldn't give him up. I pointed out that if Doucette beat Hudson, he'd almost certainly have to fight Jaffe in the second round.

"I know. But at least I'll have one win on Monday," Doucette boasted.

That was it. I would have to win six fights in order to fight Jaffe for the championship. Equally important, Jaffe would also have to win all of his six fights. Steve had been right. This was going to be a long day.

Fortunately, my first three matches were smooth sailing, although they did drain my energy. I was more concerned that my timing was off and that I lacked focus. The truth was that I won all three matches from years of ring experience and nothing more.

Two hours into the eliminations, I entered Ring 12 for my fourth match. My opponent was Dwight Stone who, although new to the circuit, was considerably younger and in superb physical condition. I jumped up and down in my corner and danced a few circles. My knees felt like worn shock absorbers trying to cushion a 250-pound sack of Portland cement, and I wasn't sure that my body was rising more than an inch or two above the floor.

Aware that I was out of shape, Stone began running the moment the referee started the match. His strategy was simple—get me to chase him for two minutes and fifty seconds, and then in the final ten seconds charge an exhausted opponent and score a quick point. I could have opted not to pursue him, but that would have triggered an onslaught of spectator booing directed at the old man that I was.

The ploy worked. After nearly three minutes of having thrown dozens of rusty kicks and punches at the quick-footed Stone, I stood flat-footed in the center of the ring, sucking air and not having scored a single point.

With only ten seconds remaining, Stone attacked with a powerful straight kick to my gut. What he didn't anticipate was my suddenly switching to his game. Retreating to the edge of the ring, I planted my rear foot and, when Stone stumbled while attempting to score a follow-up strike to my head, buried a punch into my opponent's chest. In unison the four judges yelled, "Point!" and raised their flags as the referee yelled, "Time!"

Waiting on the sidelines, the BKF cheered my arrival. Gulping water, I had only one concern—Jaffe's progress. Steve had been keeping tabs on Jaffe and informed me that he also had won his fourth round match.

I had hoped for an easier match in my next fight and was alarmed by the sight of Ken Fujimoto, a Japanese Shotokan stylist, making his way into the ring. In contrast to the soft, Chinese styles, Shotokan was a hard style, whose practitioners focused everything on delivering a series of basic killing blows. I knew that from the instant the match began, Fujimoto would charge straight at me with an assault that would be so overwhelming that the best defense was to stop the kicks and punches dead in their tracks. The huge downside to this was that, through barbaric training methods, Shotokan practitioners notoriously had arms and legs of steel.

Throughout the first two minutes of the match, blocking Fujimoto's kicks and punches was like smashing my arms against the hull of a battleship. Equally devastating were his blocks to my counterpunches and kicks. I blocked with such impact that I feared my bones would break, yet managed to score with a handsword to Fujimoto's neck and a quick groin shot before running out of bounds.

Fujimoto didn't lose his focus. With the score tied at 2-2, we were called to the center of the ring with five seconds remaining. I knew that I couldn't allow the match to go into overtime. Having not trusted the flexibility of my legs, which had been compromised because of my lack of training, throughout the match I hadn't targeted a kick above Fujimoto's abdomen and hoped that he'd noticed this and grown complacent.

As the referee restarted the match, Fujimoto charged forward with an ear-piercing yell as he launched a punch-kick combination. Timing my opponent perfectly, I centered my weight over my left leg and scored a right roundhouse kick to his head. As all four judges called the point, Fujimoto punched my ribcage with such force that I was catapulted out of the ring. With pain shooting through my chest and a pulled muscle in my groin as a result of delivering the high kick, I glanced up from the floor as the referee yelled, "Time!" I'd won the match, but again paid a heavy price.

Lissie spent the early afternoon in her small garden, tending to her flowers and refilling her birdfeeders, then settled into her living room where she worked on a quilt she was making for her new grandchild. When her hands grew tired, she set the quilt aside and read her Bible. Soon she became weary and fell off to sleep to what sounded like the singing of a thousand angels that gradually faded to silence—and darkness. Sometime later a distant voice called out to her, "Lissie! Lissie!"

It was a familiar voice, yet one she hadn't heard for many years. It was the voice of Joe Williams, who appeared on the edge of the woods not far from his whiskey still. Lissie looked at Joe from the crude porch of her shack and immediately sensed her husband's concern.

"What is it, Joe?"

"Go quick!" he anxiously called out. "Our boy needs you! Go quick!"

Lissie instantly awakened from the vision. After collecting herself, she took hold of her Bible, which was still in her lap. "Dear God, dear God!"

Thirty miles away, I lay unconscious on the floor of the Long Beach Sports Arena. Moments earlier my match against Tex "Wildman" Steele had gone in my favor, and I'd out-pointed my opponent 2-0 over the first two-and-a-half minutes.

Steele was a quick-tempered redneck and a notorious brawler. Technically, while he had never lost a fight, neither had he won a championship because whenever Steele was down on points and destined for a loss, he'd purposely get disqualified for excessive contact. And this is exactly what Steele had done. Realizing he was down 2-0 with only a half-minute remaining, he intentionally kicked me in the head as I stepped out of bounds and lowered my guard after time was called. Steele was not only disqualified for excessive contact, but he was ejected from the tournament.

Later, I lay on a table in one of the several dressing rooms. A bright light stabbed into my right eye, then my left, and I could smell the stale breath of the aging tournament physician who hovered over me. I could sense there were others in the room.

"His pupils appear even," the doctor said. He had earlier tested my motor reflexes and taken my blood pressure, which were normal. "What day is it, Mr. Williams?"

"Today is the worst day of Dave Jaffe's life," I haughtily replied, my head throbbing.

"No. I need the day of the week."

"Saturday."

"Who is the President of the United States?"

"Some rich white dude. Why else do you think he lives in the White House?" I said with an attitude that drew laughter from my BKF comrades.

The door opened and my mother entered the room. She hurried to my side and cuddled my head. "Oh, my baby, my baby!"

"Momma!" I replied, surprised to see her.

She turned to the doctor. "What's wrong with my baby?"

"He appears to be all right. Just took a blow to the head."

Momma was relieved. It wasn't the first time I'd been hit during competition.

"Momma, what are you doing here?"

"God has sent me. He spoke to me through…" She hesitated telling me about my father having appeared to her in a vision.

"Through who, Momma?" I probed.

"Why are you fighting? You supposed to be retired."

"I had to, Momma."

"I understand," she replied knowingly.

"You do?"

"Yes. I feel God want you here."

"Really?"

"Yes, child. God know what's best for His children."

"Glory be to God," I said, gleaming with the belief that God intended for me to put some serious hurt on this disrespectful honky. Somehow I sensed that my mother didn't quite see it that way.

chapter eleven

The Championship

After being released by the tournament doctor, I returned to the arena. It came as no surprise that Dave Jaffe was the heavy favorite to make short work of me in our upcoming championship fight. Practically everyone outside the BKF was complaining that the fight was a horrible mismatch and that my reaching the finals was nothing more than luck.

Ten minutes later I sat alone in the darkened upper tier of the arena, looking down at the elevated staging where in 20 minutes I would fight for the world karate championship. Early bird spectators were beginning to take their seats; food and drink vendors were gearing up to peddle their wares to a packed house; and film crews were running cables and adjusting sound and lighting.

I knew that my only chance of victory was to enliven my primal fighting spirit—to tap into my racial hatred. After several deep breaths, I closed my eyes and mentally relived the countless dehumanizing childhood memories of growing up as a Negro boy in the Jim Crow South. I brought up mental pictures of the abject poverty my mother and siblings had been forced to endure, the five white Marines who savagely beat me in Vietnam, and the karate instructor in Kingsville, Texas, who charged me higher dues and allowed one of his black belts to refer to me as "the nigger." I recalled my years in the black ghetto community of Rocktown and the night James Vaughn drove off in my momma's car with most of her worldly belongings and meager savings, leaving us destitute. And finally, I relived the events of that morning when Dave Jaffe publicly humiliated and vilified me by laughing in my face and calling me a has-been in front of the martial arts community.

While in previous years tapping into my anger resulted in my shifting to a primal survival mode, for the first time ever it acted in reverse. Instead of quickening my heart rate, raising my blood pressure, and pouring adrenaline into my arteries, my mind and body gradually began to feel like a hundred-year-old man. My eyesight and hearing diminished, my muscles lost their strength, and my mind lapsed into an ill-defined limbo. Just as I began to sense an eerie, almost supernatural departure of my life force, I felt someone sit beside me and take my hand. It was a familiar hand, one that I remembered as a child. I opened my eyes and looked at my mother.

"Momma," is all I could utter.

"Yes, child, it's Momma. Child, I know what is happening to you. Sooner or later this happens to all of God's children."

I felt comforted by her presence, yet couldn't talk.

"God is speaking to you, Son, and He can help you if you will simply ask Him. Walking alone is not normal. To be away from the Father's house is not normal. All you need do is come home and you'll find that God has always been there. It's just you that has been away."

She put her arms around me and rocked me like a baby, humming a song I recalled from my childhood. I suddenly felt secure and comforted, and at that moment I wished we were back in Liberty City. Even being in that old shack we lived in would have beat the Sports Arena under the circumstances I faced, and especially the way I felt inside.

Momma had always been my rock. Never in my life had she misled me. Even when I refused to listen to her wisdom, I knew that her counsel was based on her own life's experience. God had always been stronger than any obstacle she ever faced in life.

When she was finished, I stood and said, "Thank you, Momma. I need some time alone."

"I understand, child."

I kissed her cheek and made my way to a remote upstairs men's room. After observing the entrance for a while, and assured that the bathroom was empty, I slipped inside.

I was alone. Scanning the row of wash basins and urinals, I entered the farthest stall from the entrance and closed the door. I kneeled to the floor, folded my hands and bowed my head, then began with a faint whisper, "God . . . my momma has prayed her whole life. Since I was a child, I've seen you help her when she didn't have the rent, or the lights were turned off, or there wasn't any food, or we were sick. Even after both her husbands left, she raised us kids by herself, and she never complained, not once in her life, because she said that you answered all her prayers. She always taught me that you would answer mine, too, if I was to ask you. So I guess now I'm asking, because I don't know what else to do. I'm not asking for a fancy car or a mansion, nothing like that. And I'm not sick. Just plain scared, and I'm not sure why. This guy Jaffe is good, Lord. I mean real good. I've seen him fight, and he's tough— so tough that I know I can't do this without you. It's not about winning the trophy or being crowned the world karate champion. I don't care about that, and that's the truth. I got to whup this guy to get some dignity—I mean the kind Steve Sanders has, not the kind I try to convince folks I got. I'm hurting, Lord. Every bone and muscle is hurting, and I don't have much strength left. But nothing hurts more than my lack of pride. Just help me whup this guy, Lord. Please—just help me get some dignity, and I promise I will help do your work. For the rest of my life, if you will answer this one prayer, I promise I will serve you. Thank you, Father. Amen."

I remained crouched over the toilet, my hands clenched in a death grip. After a few moments, a peculiar warmth came over me, and I thought I heard the loud drumming I recalled as a child walking to the First Christ Holiness Church of Savannah. This was followed by a peaceful twilight sleep that fell upon me as the drumming gradually subsided, only to be abruptly replaced by the loudspeaker that blared from the main arena, "Mr. Williams to the center ring! Mr. Williams to the center ring—please!"

As I appeared on the upper tier walkway and started down the stairs, I saw the announcer standing in the middle of the main ring, scanning the area and talking into his microphone, "Mr. Williams to the center ring, please!"

Dave Jaffe, the tournament promoter Ed Parker, and Steve were also in the main ring. It was clear that I was moments from being disqualified, and I could see Steve pleading for a few more minutes.

The spectators had grown restless. Aside from their perceived mismatch, many wanted to see this racist loudmouth take a real whuppin' and applauded when I finally appeared at ringside, climbed into the ring and joined the others.

"Sorry about the delay. I had some important business."

Jaffe sneered at me and remarked, "Sure you did. I figured you ducked out. Be just like you."

I looked back at Jaffe and saw him as an entirely different person. I didn't notice the color of his skin. His comment didn't even bother me. I looked beyond and saw a man who had trained all year and fought all day to now give me his best. I knew I was about to fight a true champion. "I wouldn't disrespect you that way, Dave," I said sincerely.

Jaffe gave me a perplexed look and probably thought my remark was part of my strategy.

The announcer addressed the crowd. Many had begun to chant and stomp their feet. "May we have it quiet, please! Please, let us get started!" After the crowd quieted, the announcer continued, "This is the final match to determine this year's world champion! Fighters ready?"

Jaffe and I nodded and moved to the center of the ring and faced each other as Ed Parker and the announcer left the stage.

We were joined by the ref, who spoke briefly, "Let's keep it clean, gentlemen, and watch your control."

I turned to Jaffe. "Good luck to you, Dave. Let's give the crowd a good match." I held out my fist for the ritual touching, but Jaffe ignored the gesture.

"Oh, they'll get a good match, all right, as one-sided as it's going to be," he said with haughty arrogance, although seemingly curious as to why I wasn't offering up my usual verbal sparring.

Seconds before the match began, I noticed a dramatic change in me. There was no question in my mind that God had answered my prayer and had miraculously rejuvenated my body. The aches and pains were gone, and my energy level had been restored. More vivid was the absence of my usual hostility and hatred toward any white opponent I'd fought over the years. Instead, I felt compassion and camaraderie toward the man I was facing for the world championship. I wondered if this was the beginning of my feeling pride and dignity, which had eluded me throughout my life.

As heavyweights, this was truly a clash of Titans. From the second the match started we locked horns and traded points in rapid succession. White flags flew, then red flags. On several occasions, points were scored simultaneously and canceled each other out. We stepped up the contact, until Jaffe delivered a punch to my face that drew blood.

The ref immediately moved between us and held his arms outstretched. "Stop! That was excessive contact, Mr. Jaffe!" He turned to the scorekeeper, "Deduct two points from the white corner!"

Jaffe's school was furious, the BKF elated. Jaffe moved to the ref to object, but I beat him to it. "It wasn't excessive, Ref. Really. It looked worse than it was."

"It isn't up for debate, Mr. Williams," the ref replied with authority. "Fighters, let's go!"

I wasn't going to win this way. Moments after the fight resumed, I purposely dropped my lead guard, allowing Jaffe to score an easy point. Four white flags went up as the ref got between us. "Point! Stop!"

I glanced over at ringside and saw the look on Steve's face. He knew that I'd intentionally allowed Jaffe to score a point. He shook his head in disbelief, hoping I wouldn't do that again.

The fight resumed, and again I purposely opened my defense, giving Jaffe another easy score.

"Point! Stop!"

I glanced at Steve. He smiled back, knowing that I'd never be content beating Jaffe on point deductions for excessive contact.

Jaffe and I stood in the middle of the ring. Jaffe knew that he hadn't earned the last two points. Regardless of whether he knew my reasons, he surely sensed from my demeanor that the free points were over. The ref held his hand outstretched between us. "Okay, we're tied again. Ten seconds, gentlemen, unless you want to go to overtime."

At that moment, I didn't care who won. Jaffe and I were enmeshed in a dance that made us both look and feel good. If I couldn't win this race, I was determined to make Jaffe break the record. I smiled at the ref and said, "It ain't up to us. It's in God's hands now."

The ref dropped his hand, signaling the fight to resume. Jaffe and I stalked each other, exchanging shots that fell short. With two seconds remaining, I swept Jaffe off his feet, turning his body 180 degrees and catapulting him five feet off the ground. As his upward motion reached its apex, I delivered a controlled punch to his chest, directly over his heart.

"Point red!" the ref yelled.

Four red flags flew and the bell rang, ending the match. The fight was over. The crowd cheered and applauded loudly as Jaffe and I moved to the center of the ring. After our ritualistic bow, Jaffe said, "Hell of a fight, Donnie, and those two points didn't go unnoticed."

"I'd like to think you'd have done the same for me."

"What was that all about, anyway?"

"I don't know. I guess for the first time in my life I was being a proud black man," I replied. I wondered if he noticed the tears in my eyes.

Jaffe could tell I was speaking from the heart. "I'll tell you, you've got my respect," he replied sincerely.

"That goes both ways … brother."

After a thoughtful moment, Jaffe shook my hand, smiled and said, "Brother."

As I was awarded the grand champion trophy, I looked out over the spectators and no longer saw our differences. Our skin color didn't matter. Nor did the amount of money we had, the style of clothes we wore, where we lived, or the cars we drove. Instead, in my eyes we had returned to what God always intended each and every one of us to be—His children.

Epilogue

After I won the grand championship at the Long Beach Internationals, I gained immediate notoriety, which renewed my burning desire for fame and material wealth. As a result, and almost without realizing it, I forgot about my promise to God that I would serve Him for the rest of my life.

For the next several years I invested all of my time building up my martial arts schools, working as a physical trainer and therapist, and pursuing an acting career. Although I was able to pay my bills, fame and wealth eluded me, and I felt once again that I was back at square one. As a result, my anger toward white people returned.

Then in late 1979 I appeared at a karate tournament to which comedian Richard Pryor had attached his name because the event was billed as a fundraiser for "March Against Drugs." After the event ended, I was interviewed by a reporter from the LA Times. I recalled how two years earlier I'd appeared at the Internationals as a judge and not a competitor, and how I'd won the championship after praying to God kneeling before a toilet.

After making a few notes, the reporter glanced up from his notepad and asked, "So what have you done since promising God that you'd serve him for the rest of your life?" The question caught me by surprise, and all I could say was that I hadn't done anything—yet.

Years passed and I couldn't get that reporter's question off my mind. It just wouldn't go away. Eventually, I told my wife that I felt that the Lord was calling me. I had no idea what that meant and even less of an idea as to what I was supposed to do about it. So I did the only thing I knew I could do—I prayed.

A few weeks later, a young man invited me to give a sermon at his church. I'd never given a sermon before, and so I asked my pastor what he thought I should do. He was very supportive and felt that the invitation was God putting me on a course that would allow me to finally honor my earlier promise.

The Sunday morning that I gave my sermon, I was nervous. I was standing at the pulpit instead of sitting with the congregation. Today I can't recall the subject of my sermon, which I gave nearly 25 years ago, although I do recall abandoning my notes about halfway through and preaching from my heart.

When the service was over, many of the church members told me that as they watched me give my sermon, it was clearly evident that I became filled with the Holy Spirit and that God was speaking through me. Over the next several months, I was invited back to that church to preach and was eventually offered the position of church pastor, which I gladly accepted.

Almost immediately several things began to happen. First, I began to have less and less interest in any business endeavors outside the church. And, second, almost like clockwork, my anger and hatred toward white people subsided. I began spending the majority of my time fixing up the church, and even went so far as to take my own couch from my home and put it in my new "Pastor's Office."

When I began preaching, I had no previous formal education in theology. I just loved God and, thanks to my mother's many years of taking me to church and reading to me from the Bible, had a good understanding of God's Word of Salvation.

In my heart, I didn't feel this was enough, and so I began taking classes in theology at the International Gospel Assembly, whose headquarters are located in Springfield, Missouri. Over time, my passion to become a biblical scholar was surpassed only by my passion for God.

When I accepted the position of pastor of the church, my own pastor had told me that he felt that God was putting me on a path to fulfill my promise to serve Him for the rest of my life. As things turned out, God didn't intend for my path to end at that church because as its membership grew, so did a subtle friction between me and the man who'd offered me the position of pastor. While the individual points we differed on weren't monumental, collectively they resulted in my leaving the church, carrying my couch on my back.

Over the next several months I became despondent. I missed the church, and even my interest in the martial arts waned, and I ended up giving away my trophies. More importantly, I missed preaching. I felt dead inside and no longer felt that I had a purpose. Then one by one the church elders and deacons, who missed me as much as I missed them, began stopping by my home where we began holding Sunday services and Bible studies in my living room. When our group grew to eight members, I became concerned that there wasn't room for those who wanted to join us. Not knowing how I could remedy this, I did the only thing I knew I could do—I prayed.

Clearly God heard my prayer because it wasn't long thereafter that I was led to a large vacant commercial building that was for sale in Pasadena. The building was anything but the Crystal Cathedral. In fact, for many years it had been a popular auto repair shop. The place was the size of a small airplane hangar, had a thick coat of grease on the concrete floor, battered walls, and reeked of oil. Of all the things it didn't have that resembled a church, it did have the only thing I wanted—it had presence of God.

With the help of the Lord and those eight people who were meeting in my living room, I purchased that building and over many months turned it into a beautiful church. Through the years we've been there, people stop by to see the old auto repair shop where they used to bring their cars for repairs.

I'm always proud to give them a tour that ends in our main sanctuary where they stand in amazement and often comment, "Bishop Williams, I can't believe what you've done to this place." For years I've had the same response. I smile and say, "My friend, I didn't do anything. God did this."

I eventually completed my studies through the International Gospel Assembly, whose president personally came to my church and bestowed upon me a doctorate in theology. Today I'm the head pastor of The Family Church International located in Pasadena, California, as well as overseeing three other churches in Modesto, Monrovia, and Fresno, California. My ultimate goal is to establish new churches throughout the country, and I'm confident that, with God's help, The Family Church will succeed in founding five new churches over the next ten years.

In 2004 my mother passed away quietly in her sleep at the age of 82 and was buried beside her mother in Pembroke, Georgia. While I miss her dearly, I'm comforted in knowing that she's at peace, having returned to her Father's home, which is an event she looked forward to throughout her life.

Although I searched for my biological father for many years, I never found him. Because he was 55 years old when I was born, he's now gone. When my mother passed, my sister discovered letters that he'd written to our mother when he was in his seventies and employed on a merchant marine ship. Although in my heart I will always love him, I continue to have mixed feelings and many questions about the life and death of Joe Williams.

As the result of my wife and my continual prayers, her father finally accepted me into his family. Over the course of 25 years we became the best of friends. Albert Juarez, whom I called "Pop," passed away in 2003.

Today I know that I'm a blessed man. While I never acquired a big mansion in Beverly Hills, I live in a beautiful home that I truly love. And while I don't drive a new half-million dollar Rolls

Royce, I love the car that I do drive. Of all the blessings God has given to me, those I cherish most are my loving wife, our five wonderful and healthy children, Donnie, Jr., Gina, Charles, Steve, and Chaaz, and our ten grandchildren.

Beginning that day in the Long Beach Sports Arena, my life has made a complete turnaround because of the relationship I have with Jesus. The positive changes in me have been remarkable. What follows in the second part of this book is my understanding of how these things occurred, as well as why they had to occur. I hope that you will find these insights to be as valuable to you as they have been to me.

Happy moments, praise God.
Difficult moments, seek God.
Quiet moments, worship God.
Painful moments, trust God.
Every moment, thank God.

PART TWO

The Renewal of the Mind

chapter twelve

The Problem of Separation

The best definition I've ever heard for insanity is "repeating the same behaviors expecting different results." If your negative thoughts and actions are causing your life to be less than you want it to be, then you have first to identify and change your wrong thinking, and then change your actions to create a positive change in your life. Put another way, you cannot change what you don't acknowledge. In order to change my self-image, I first had to acknowledge that it needed changing. You can do this by listening to the inner voice that prompted you to read this book in the first place.

My Problem Was More Than Simply Not Liking White People

For many years I was identified as a racist, both by others and by myself. But when I took a closer look into what I had become, I realized that my anger and hatred were the result of something much broader than racism because in reality I didn't hate all white people. Prior to marrying Valerie, I was married to a white woman, following a long relationship. I also named my son Steven Carlos Williams after Chuck Norris.

So clearly my anger wasn't specific to white people. Instead, I resented all people and situations that made me feel like a loser. If I drove past a mansion in Beverly Hills, I was angry that someone else was living in it, and the color of that person's skin didn't matter. If a Rolls Royce passed by, I was angry because someone else was driving that car when that car should have more rightfully belonged to me. And if a person were highly educated, I became resentful because I didn't have a college education. I could add appreciably to this list.

So eventually I had to recognize that white people weren't the cause of my anger. It was just easier to blame them for everything. As you read what follows, it would help for you to make a list of everything that causes you ill feeling—be that people, places, things, or situations.

If you're like me, and I presume that you are, you'll ultimately discover that nothing on your list is the problem—the problem is within you. When I knelt before that toilet in Long Beach, I asked God to give me the strength to be victorious over another person, but what I really wanted was for God to give *me* some dignity.

My Initial Turning Away from God

Beginning early in my childhood and continuing on into my adult years, I saw God only as a provider of material things. Moreover, from my perspective, God and I were worlds apart. Our distant, if not nonexistent, relationship was similar to the one I had with my biological father Joe Williams. While I knew I had a father, I never met him, or even saw him at a distance. All I had was that tiny black and white photo, which my mother showed me just before I joined the Navy. Because the photo was faded and torn in places, it was difficult for me to get a sense of my father's identity, which is the same problem I had defining God.

Besides having little understanding of who or where God was, I believed that His purpose was simply to provide material things. That was it. That's what I saw. People who were blessed by God drove nice cars and lived in nice homes with televisions. Those whom God chose not to bless either traveled by bus or walked and lived in shacks.

The god my momma saw was different from mine. To her, God provided only the bare living necessities, yet blessed His followers with spiritual gifts such as peace of mind and a meaningful purpose in life. So although it was clear to me that my momma lived her life based on her complete, unconditional faith and trust in God, I didn't see God doing anything for her because she didn't have anything material. Our family lived in squalor, and for years my momma worked hard cleaning people's houses and working in the school cafeteria for a meager check. Prior to moving to California, my momma never owned a car and never bought a dress for herself.

Every Sunday I wore ugly shoes and hand-me-downs to church. My life didn't match what I was seeing on TV, and although my friend Jeremy told me that what I was seeing wasn't real, I didn't believe him until I came to California. Here I discovered the lives of countless numbers of blacks who lived in ghettos like Rocktown. And so I had to wonder where God was.

From everything I saw around me, and the way I felt inside, He certainly wasn't providing anything material in my life. If God's plan was for me to live out my life in poverty, I didn't need Him. I felt that I could do a better job taking care of myself—and in time I planned to take care of my momma by providing her a big home, a nice car, and plenty of money in the bank. To my way of thinking, her peace of mind would be dramatically increased if she could buy herself a nice dress and didn't have to scrub floors and walk to work.

We all have our crosses to bear in life. Mine was that I was born into a world of oppression and prejudice. I didn't create the unfair world I was born into. The Jim Crow laws had been in place long before I arrived. These laws defined more than my thoughts and my actions; they defined my place in society—my past, present, and, more importantly my future. I wasn't worthy of being educated or living in a comfortable home or driving a nice car or even earning a decent wage. The dreams I had of making something of my life weren't worth a plug nickel. While America may have been the Land of Opportunity, to a black kid living in poverty in Savannah, Georgia, America was the Land of No Opportunity.

As a child I accepted my inferior station in life as representative of who I truly was—and wasn't. The television that I watched at my friend Jeremy's home and the fact that my father had abandoned me at birth, and that I had no mentors further compounded my sense of being isolated. By the time I left Savannah, Georgia, I had begun to make the terrible mistake of comparing how I saw myself with how I saw others.

The seeds of my feeling unworthy and different from a major part of society continued to grow throughout my life, sometimes by leaps and bounds. By the time I reached the age of 30, I fully understood the words of Sartre, who defined hell as "other people." That first Sunday in August 1977, when I knelt in front of that toilet at the Long Beach Sports Arena, was the lowest point in my life, but I hadn't gotten to that place overnight. It took me the better part of 30 years to finally ask God for help.

It's an irony of life that oftentimes we can learn as much about living from the person who shows us what *not* to do as we can from the person who shows us what *to do*. Put another way, we can learn as much from what we reject as we can from what we accept. If the answers you're seeking were to be found in the places you've been looking, you would have already found them and most likely wouldn't have any need to read this book.

My initial solution to my problem of feeling separated from others, from God, and ultimately from myself resulted in total failure. Perhaps by sharing with you my experience from traveling along the wrong road, you'll be able to recognize this and, if you're on that same road, make a hard U-turn and redirect your life's course.

My first response to feeling less worthy than everyone else was to try to gain approval by doing as I was told because I truly didn't know how to fight the system. As a child, I wore that white T-shirt and tied that tie around my neck because I felt to do so made me look successful, even though my brother laughed at me and my momma scolded me for not wearing proper clothes to church. When I walked down the streets of Savannah, I stepped aside for white people because I felt to do so would make me fit in, even though I never got a thank you. When I attended school in California, I asked my teacher to help me with my reading problem so that I'd be like the other kids, but was ignored. And in order to win the approval of the gang, I tried learning how to fight by taking up karate and ended up getting slugged in the face.

Trying to fix my insides by aligning my outsides to be acceptable to others simply didn't work and never would have because there would always be an endless string of new people to please. People who live this way are forced to forever adjust their existence, as well as their perceptions of themselves. Gaining the approval of a class of people who make $25,000 a year results in our facing a new class of people who make $35,000 per year. When it became clear that I was fighting a losing battle, I gave up this strategy and adopted a more dramatic approach.

If You Can't Join Them, Beat Them

While my initial approach of pleasing others came with a pleasant veneer of agreeability and a smile, my new approach was fueled by anger, blame, and judgment, which was geared toward one purpose—I was going to prove them wrong!

Renowned philosopher Eric Hofer once pointed out that you can discover what your enemy fears the most by observing the means he uses to frighten you.

By the time I reached my early teens, I was convinced that the main goal of the Jim Crow laws was simply to keep me down financially. The message was that money and power go hand-in-hand. I wasn't going to receive a good education unless someone paid for it. And I wasn't going to live in a decent neighborhood and drive a decent car unless I could obtain a good paying job and pay for these things. It was a vicious circle, a catch-22, because I would never land a decent job without an education, which for a black kid living in Georgia and then in the ghetto in California, was going to be impossible. So in my mind, what white people feared was that I would achieve financial success and, because of my money, gain power over them—all of which is exactly what I set out to do.

When I was a child, my intention wasn't to shove my future acquisition of money down the throats of white people, but throwing my success in their faces was my intention by the time I'd been in California for a short while. And that remained my intention right up until that moment when I knelt before that toilet in Long Beach.

Identifying my motivation is easy to see in retrospect. In the early 1970s when I found that I had a wad of money, I didn't give it to the church. Instead, I purchased a used limousine, restored it to mint condition, and then parked it in the red zone outside the Long Beach Sports Arena. And when some snotty nosed, white parking attendant told me that I had to move it, I had one of my entourage tell him on no uncertain terms that Donnie Williams parked his car wherever he pleased.

At my insistence, whenever the BKF fighting team walked into a tournament, we wore our power on our sleeves and dared people to object. Every chance I got, I fueled the media's belief that the BKF was to be feared because we were connected with the Black Panthers and the notorious black street gangs of the inner cities.

Donnie Williams was going to be in control of the world, which included every situation and everyone connected to any situation. I controlled men—particularly white men—by instilling fear in them through my martial arts prowess. With women, I controlled them through my charm and sexual prowess. If a woman played hard to get with me, as I initially felt that Valerie did, I'd stay on her until she capitulated.

My life was all about controlling my environment simply because taking charge of everything and everyone was the only way I saw of becoming a millionaire—and becoming rich was the only way I felt people would ever accept me because it seemed to me that everyone connected a person's worth with success, and they connected success with money.

The Illusion of Fame and Fortune

My belief that acquiring wealth would result in "fitting in" didn't work any better than my initial plan to please everyone. Changing my outer environment had little effect on my self-worth. Although I did achieve a degree of material success and notoriety, I was painting over rust because all I really succeeded in doing was to widen the divide between myself and the people I was trying to win over.

It didn't matter what I did. In my mind, the party I was at wasn't where the real party was, which was always down the street or on the other side of town or on another continent. Somehow I always sensed that white people knew that the image I was presenting to them was an act, only they weren't telling me. Although I rode in luxury cars and dressed the way successful people dress, I still felt like that poor black kid in Savannah walking to church wearing those oversized clothes and black shoes that looked to be anything but black and were held together by clothes hanger wire. I just couldn't figure out why I kept feeling so disconnected.

Trying to either please everyone or make people accept me because I looked successful made people uncomfortable because it was clear that I was never content with anything for very long. By having to constantly gear my actions to what I perceived as the thoughts and opinions of others, I gave others the impression that I didn't know what I wanted and that my desires were limitless and ever-changing. For years this was the way I came off to people, and it made them uncomfortable to the degree that they didn't know how to deal with me. Nothing satisfies an individual who is incapable of the simple activity of enjoying his or her own life.

Worst of all, deep inside I began to realize that it was going to be impossible for me to feel compassion for others if I were to succeed in forcefully driving a wedge between myself and them. When I was a child, my momma pointed to a verse in the Bible to which I should have paid attention—"Not by might nor by power, but by My Word, saith the Lord."

Years ago a close friend said to me, "Donnie, I've been very rich in my day, and I've been very poor, and the only difference I've noticed is that when I've been rich, I eat a better cut of meat and sleep in a better bed." And then he added, "I found out that just because I sleep in a better bed doesn't mean that I'm going to sleep any better. Some of the best sleep I've had was on an old lumpy sofa during my broke college years, and some of the worst nights I've had were when I slept in a four-poster bed in my million dollar house."

Jesus said the same thing when He said, "Who by taking thought can add one cubit to his stature?" What He meant was that while you can change everything that is a reflection of how you and others perceive your outer being—your car, your home, your friends, your wife, and your bank account—none of these things will change the reality of your inner being.

You can alter practically everything in your life, but you can't change the fact that you're going to wake up every morning to yourself. Those feet you walk on are going to carry you around for the rest of your life.

MY PLANS DEFEATED

It's an alarming fact that statistically more people die in this country every year from suicide than from murder. The relevant message is that collectively as a society we hate ourselves more than we hate others.

Earlier I quoted Eric Hofer, who said that you can discover what your enemy fears most by observing the means he uses to frighten you. In my earlier discussion, I implied that initially my enemy was white people. However, I believe that Hofer's words suggest that white people weren't the only soldiers on the battlefield.

In August 1977 when I was publicly berated on the main floor of the Long Beach Sports Arena, I later came to recognize that there were two enemies there that day—first, the person who lashed out at me and, second, myself. The harsh words said to me triggered my anger because I feared the possibility that there was truth in what was said. On that day, I'd come to Long Beach with no intention of competing because I hadn't trained in months, and I'd been beating myself up for a long time for being out of shape.

The Enemy Within

Sometimes we believe that we can improve ourselves by a cruel system of self-condemnation. The slogan is, "You, too, can hate yourself into being a better person." The people who say, "I hate myself because I'm unattractive!" are doing themselves a great disservice. The fact is that being unloving toward yourself will never result in a positive change. Unloving words and thoughts are a form of hate, and it doesn't matter if unkindness is directed at others or yourself. On the day that I competed for the world championship, I'd gone beyond being angry at others and with God. I'd begun to treat myself in an unloving way.

I stated earlier that running my life based on negative thoughts, beliefs, and actions resulted in my feeling separated from others, from God, and ultimately from myself. In a sense, within my own being I'd given birth to a spiritual cancer that eventually would have killed the God in me, as well my own spirit, in the process. If you're feeling increasingly separated from the world in which you live, the only solution is to do what I did and ask God for help.

I Tried Running the Show My Way and Failed

Prior to developing a satisfactory relationship with God, I'd always been the type of person who found my own answers to my own problems. Unfortunately, all too often, every time I found an answer to a problem, the result was a worse state of affairs than what I had before my brilliant idea. So for me, a constellation of events had to collide in order for me to finally quit trying to solve my own problems.

For the better part of 30 years I tried running my life by myself. While I occasionally accepted help from others, I was the one who decided to accept their help, which meant that I was still in charge. Before that moment when I sat with my momma in the stands of the Long Beach Sports Arena and headed for that men's room, I'd used up every resource I had at my disposal, and while I won a few battles, I lost the war. If there was any way in the world that I could have avoided kneeling before that toilet, I would have tried it. Up until that moment when I became convinced that I'd completely run out of alternative plans, there was absolutely no way in the universe that anyone was going to convince me to ask God for help. Even when our convoy was ambushed and I was fired upon in Vietnam, I didn't pray to God to get me out alive. In fact, praying never occurred to me.

Surrender

My accepting that I'd failed as the Commander-in-Chief of running the war of my life was a blessing. And I gave a great sigh of relief upon realizing that I didn't have to create a new Monday morning battle strategy. The war of life was over, and all the soldiers could leave their guns and cannons on the battlefield and return home.

For a full decade prior to surrendering my life to the Lord, I'd waged many wars within the martial arts community, as well as in the battle arenas of the karate tournament circuit. Throughout my years of martial arts training, I heard other martial artists quote the father of Japanese karate, Gichin Funakoshi, who said, "The ultimate aim in the art of karate lies not in victory but in the perfection of the characters of its participants." While I often heard this passage, I never reflected on its meaning. Looking back at my many years of karate competition, I recognize that while I won many battles, there wasn't any character in an inanimate trophy, no more so than there would be in a six-figure bank account or an expensive Italian suit.

You Cannot Serve Two Masters

In Matthew 6:24, Jesus says, "No one can serve two masters; for either he will hate the one and love the other, or else he will be loyal to the one and despise the other. You cannot serve God and mammon." In the Bible, mammon means riches, which the Bible defines as "things of this world," which in common day terminology includes the lust for and seeking of "people, places, and things."

Like many others, the trap that I fell into was that I believed that wealth would shield me from the reality of my spiritual poverty and lack of dependence on God. Failing to acquire fame and fortune turned out to be a blessing because it made it impossible for me to maintain the illusion of control and easier for me to see my need for God.

As long as a person relies on money to provide security in life, God will continue to take a second seat. In the Bible, Jesus clearly states that pursuing the kingdom of God and righteous living are to remain our top priorities. "But seek first the kingdom of God and His righteousness, and all these things will be added to you." (Matthew 6:33). Given the choice of relying on God or money to provide security in your life, I am living proof that God is infinitely better qualified and far more consistent.

I Couldn't Fix Myself

If you're going to fix a problem, it helps a great deal if you know what the problem is. For years, I was like a man who was trying to figure out why he couldn't keep heat in his house and kept calling the heating repairman to check the furnace instead of calling a roofer, who would have pointed out that the house didn't have a roof.

A person who has a toothache goes to a dentist. Someone who suffers from acne or needs a heart transplant seeks out the services of a medical doctor. People who are having problems with depression or having difficulty relating to their spouses seek the help of a psychologist or marriage counselor. But where do people go to seek help if they feel separated from the world in which they live? Where do they go when they don't have a workable understanding about why they're here in the first place? Where do they go when they finally recognize that what is truly ailing them cannot be fixed through any human resource?

When I prayed to God on that day in Long Beach, I was very clear that I wasn't asking for a new car or a palatial mansion or to be healed from a terminal illness. I asked God to give me some dignity. Deep inside I knew, probably because of what my momma had been telling me since I was a child, that my problem was a spiritual problem. While human doctors could have healed my mind and body, only God has the ability to restore a person's broken spirit.

I'd been away from my Father's house for so long that I'd forgotten why and when I'd left. I suppose what I was really praying for that day was for God to allow me to come home. To this day, whenever I recall that day in Long Beach, tears of joy well up in my eyes. In the 30 years leading up to that moment, I had never experienced a greater feeling than to know that in God's eyes I'd never really been away.

God Lifted the Weight of the World off My Shoulders

Without a doubt, the biggest fear I faced that day, particularly considering that I felt that I had nowhere else to turn, was that God either wouldn't hear my prayer or wouldn't care. Had I prayed for God's help and then taken a humiliating whupping from my opponent, I would have sunk into deeper despair, if that were even possible.

But that's not what happened. In the Book of Matthew, Jesus said, "Ask, and it shall be given to you; seek, and you shall find; knock, and it shall be opened to you. For whoever asks, receives; and he who seeks, finds; and to him who knocks, the door is opened." Jesus could not have been clearer about this message, and He meant every word of what He said.

Five minutes before I knelt to the floor of that men's room, my momma told me that all I had to do was ask God for help. She'd been saying this to me since I was a child, but I didn't believe it, even though I knew that the strength of her belief in God's ability and willingness to answer prayer was far greater than any obstacle she ever faced. What my momma also knew was that the words that Jesus spoke were true only if I believed them.

In the Book of Matthew, Jesus tells His following that if they had the faith of a grain of mustard seed, they could tell a mountain to "Move from here to there" and it would move, and that *nothing would be impossible to them as long as they believed.*

What Is True in Your Life Is Only What You Acknowledge to Be True

My lack of faith was what kept me from allowing God to work in my life. While the Word of God has always been the complete truth, the Word had no meaning in reality until I acknowledged it as being true.

This basic premise worked in all areas of my life, not only my belief in God. For example, the Jim Crow laws were based on many falsehoods, but because I believed them to be true, they became a very real part of my reality for many years.

The plain and simple truth is that your world is based entirely on what you, yourself, acknowledge to be true, regardless of whether it's true or not or whether anyone agrees with you or not. This is clearly illustrated in the Book of Proverbs where it states that "As a man thinketh in his heart so is he." If a person chooses to believe that God doesn't answer prayers, or even that God doesn't exist, then in *their* world God truly neither answers prayers nor exists, even though He exists and answers prayers in the worlds of many others.

chapter thirteen

God's Solution - Success

Years ago, a reporter who was interviewing Ray Charles asked, "What is the worst part about being blind?" to which Ray responded, "Well, you can't see." Oftentimes it is the most obvious and simplest answer that eludes us.

There's a hard way and an easy way to live life. The hard way is to arise each morning and face the world by yourself—to spend your waking hours worrying over keeping a roof over your head, food on the table, shoes on your kids' feet, and hoping that through your personal actions and guidance all of your loved ones and friends are happy and healthy. The easy way is to join in a partnership with God and allow Him to take full responsibility for your concerns, which in turn assures that your efforts will create the best results.

Walking Alone Is Not Natural

God never meant for us to spend a lifetime walking alone. The Word of God makes it abundantly clear that, from the cradle to the grave, God wants to be a major part of our lives.

For the better part of 30 years I walked alone and faced life by myself. I put forth my best efforts and ended up like the Prodigal Son shoveling manure in a pig farm. Then in August 1977 I prayed for God to take charge of my life, and since that moment my life has never been so good. And the amazing part is that since allowing God into my life, I haven't had to work anywhere near as hard as I was, and the blessings I've received are a hundredfold.

Imagine your boss at work telling you that you're going to work a much shorter work week for ten times the pay. When I began serving God and made Him the boss, this is exactly what happened. It's beautiful.

Affirm Your Belief in God and Begin to Dramatically Change Your Life

Sooner or later each of us has to arrive at a decision that God either exists or He does not. The simple and conclusive answer to this question can be found in the basic nature of human behavior.

As humans we reproduce ourselves through our seeds of male sperm and female eggs. If it weren't for this continual planting of our seeds, the human race would cease to exist. In a similar fashion, God reproduces Himself by planting a need for God in every new human being.

Since the beginning of creation, human beings—regardless of where they reside on earth or the nature of their religious and spiritual beliefs—have a profound need to define and seek a supreme power of the universe, which many refer to as God. That billions of people who have lived on earth since creation have experienced this need isn't surprising. We seem to know intuitively that the universe is simply too ordered and complex for there not to exist a form of creative intelligence that is unfathomably greater than ourselves.

For hundreds of years many religious and spiritual leaders have uttered variations of an ancient Indian wisdom that says, "That which you are seeking is causing you to seek." The fact that humans naturally have a deep inner *need* for God and, based on that need, *seek* God throughout their lifetime is convincing proof that God exists. While we actively seek God, it is the seed of God planted in us by God that is causing our need to seek Him. Again, planting this need in us is how God reproduces Himself. Without our *need* for God, He would cease to be.

Those who believe in the nonexistence of God and that they live in a world without order are at the mercy of circumstances. Why be here if you're just the product of random outside forces? If you drift along without decision and definitive purpose, you become the helpless victim of circumstance. Belief in God and following His Word is the proven remedy to nullifying this feeling of utter helplessness.

God Is Sufficient Onto All Your Needs

When you board an airplane, you don't question whether airplanes can fly or whether the pilot knows what he's doing. You're already convinced of both; otherwise you wouldn't be on that plane. In a similar fashion, when you ask God to take control of your life, you must firmly believe that you have placed your life in good hands and that God is 100 percent capable of weathering any and all storms.

There are no shades of gray. God is either *fully* capable of taking charge of *every* aspect of your life or He isn't. If you feel that God is incapable of fulfilling all your needs, then your God is too small, and you need to take the time to come to a better understanding of the awesome power that God is.

There is no greater teacher than personal firsthand experience. Since asking God to take control of my life, He has answered every one of my prayers. Not some of them or most of them—but every one of them. God has blessed me with healthy children, a beautiful home, a loving wife, and given me my life's work as a preacher. Prior to turning my life over to God, I was an angry karate tournament fighter with little purpose in life and even less money in my pocket.

The dramatic difference in my life has been the result of my ongoing relationship with Jesus, which has been a real eye-opener. I know today that God answers prayers. I know today that God heals the sick. I know today that God honestly cares about every second of my personal life. I know today that when I go to sleep at night, God lives inside me, and I know that when I awaken, He'll still be with me. For 30 years all the changes I have undergone were right where they've always been—inside me just waiting for me first to discover them and, second, to believe that I had a God-given right to them.

Your living faith in God is based solely on the strength of your belief. "As thy faith is, so be it unto thee" is as true today as it was 2,000 years ago. It is absolute unquestioning faith that brings results. Jesus said it this way, "All things are possible to him who believes."

God meets our needs through us, not by simply giving us things, but also by providing us strength and resolve. The Bible says, "And you shall remember the Lord your God, for it is He who gives you power to get wealth that He may establish His covenant which He swore to your fathers, as it is this day." (Deuteronomy 8:18). This verse doesn't say that God gives you wealth. What it says is that God *gives you power to get* wealth, which is another way of stating that God will provide you strength and determination, but it's up to you to do the work.

You Are Uniquely Special to God

The last world census count estimated that there are presently more than six billion people living on earth. Given the highly technical, fast-paced world that we live in today, it's easy to see why so many people believe that God doesn't have time to become intimately involved with each and every one of His children. If this is your belief, you're making the mistake of perceiving God as finite rather than infinite.

I have five children and ten grandchildren, and most of the time they're each in a different location. So unless I could create 14 clones of myself, it's impossible for me to give all of my children and grandchildren my complete attention at the same time.

However, because God is infinite and not finite, He is capable of giving each of His more than six billion children His *complete* love and attention, and He can do this for eternity and without a moment's rest.

The key to understanding why God is capable of devoting His attention to each and every one of His children at the same time is to recognize that God is not a physical body that can be in only one part of the universe at one time. In the Book of John, it is written, "God is spirit." And when Jesus was asked by the woman at the well to define God, Jesus gave her the same definition—that God is spirit—and in so being, He resides equally *in* each of us. "Know ye not that you are the temple of the living God."

However intense your needs are, be assured that you will always have God's full attention. And His attention isn't anything you have to earn, and it doesn't matter if when praying to God it's your first prayer or your last. God will hear and value your prayer with the same intensity that He listens to the prayers of the Pope or heard the prayer of the thief on the Cross.

THERE IS BUT ONE FATHER

I spent years trying to find my biological father Joe Williams because I had a profound need for a protector and mentor. When I failed to find my father, I attached myself to surrogate fathers, such as Bishop Owens and others. Although my momma was a prominent figure in my life, she didn't replace the need I had for my father, and this need didn't diminish when I became an adult.

Ultimately I discovered that placing my faith and expectations in human fathers proved disappointing because sooner or later they either fell far short of my expectations or they died.

Throughout my momma's life, she consistently told me that the only father I needed was my Heavenly Father. In her mind, no mortal was ever going to have the love, understanding, and ability to meet my every need in life. It took me 30 years to discover the truth of my momma's words. Had I heeded the wisdom that she'd learned through her own living, I would have saved myself, and others, a great deal of suffering.

The Search for My Father Ended with Finding My Heavenly Father

My security and peace of mind wasn't to be found in my biological father or the string of surrogate fathers—or fame and fortune, which in a sense can be a protector and an individual's security. All I needed to do in order to acquire all the things that were missing in my life was to come home to my Heavenly Father and allow Him to take care of me.

The night our shack burned to the ground and everything we had was gone, I saw the peace in my momma's eyes when she bundled up us kids in that worn coat of hers and told us that everything was going to be all right. And she meant it. Nearly 20 years would pass before I understood that feeling when I prayed in front of that toilet in Long Beach, and God removed all my shortcomings and made me whole.

Years ago, a friend who was aware that I'd expended considerable time and effort searching for my biological father asked me, "If you had found your dad, what would you have wanted from him? What is it that you wanted to know?" After a few moments, I replied, "I wanted his approval. Every child needs his dad's approval." Because I couldn't connect with my dad, I spent years trying to win the approval of others, which was an approach to life that proved futile.

In sharp contrast, gaining the approval of God was the easiest thing I ever did. All that was necessary was for me to sincerely ask for Him to come into my life and to tell Him that I would do my best to serve Him. It was just that easy. All I had to do was to come back home, and I found that God had always been there. I was the one who had been away.

"For this my son was dead, and is alive again; he was lost, and is found. And they began to be merry." (Luke 15:24)

The parable of the Prodigal Son in the Gospel of Luke is familiar to many people. In part, it's the story of a rebellious son who rejects his upbringing. Prideful and strong, the son heads off to a faraway land where he leads a wild life of adventure and squanders everything of value. Not until he's confronted with failure and despair does he return home, repentant and willing to do anything to win back his father's favor.

The primary focus of this parable is a beautiful story of God's patient grace and His willingness to welcome each of us, His rebellious children, home into His loving and forgiving arms.

The story of the Prodigal Son is my story, and for many of you it's also your story. Since childhood, my momma provided me with a loving environment that included taking me every Sunday to church where she made certain that I was taught the Word of God. In a sense, my momma's home was an extension of God's home.

Around the time I reached my teens, I made a conscious decision to turn away from God and leave my momma's home (both figuratively and literally) in order to pursue a lifestyle that went against Christian principles and values.

The Land of Opportunity was mine for the taking. I had big plans of making a name for myself in karate, driving a Rolls Royce, rubbing shoulders with Hollywood celebrities, dressing in fancy clothes, and living in a mansion. Although my momma told me that seeking fame and fortune ultimately wouldn't serve me well, I chose not to hear her.

Had I acquired the monetary fortune I was planning on obtaining, I fully intended to use my wealth and power against white people as a means to abuse them the way they'd abused me. Not long after I made my appearance on the karate tournament circuit, I began to strut and swagger while boasting to everyone about my accomplishments, be they real or imagined.

Like the Prodigal Son, I eventually ended up wasting my substance on wrongful living. My plans to intimidate and control everything and everyone around me failed. Finding myself with nowhere else to turn and overcome with intense feelings of hopelessness, I fell to my knees and asked God if I could come home. My self-condemnation was overwhelming.

When I prayed to God for help, He could have chosen to ignore me, but He didn't. He also could have chosen to appear before me with a stern reprimand. "What is this I'm hearing? You're asking me to give you dignity, after the way you've treated your brothers and sisters—My children—for all these years? I have a good memory. Trust me. I know every time you've turned right when your mother told you to turn left. I have a list of people you've berated and tried your best to control, people whose lives you've made difficult, if not miserable. I also have a list of women you've misled and deceived in order to satisfy your own selfish needs. And now you're coming before Me asking Me to give you dignity?"

But God didn't do that either. Instead, he saw me coming down the road a half hour before I appeared in that men's room, and He sent my momma to comfort me when I was sitting high up in the stands of the arena. He sent her to sit beside me and hold my hand, and asked her to rock me and sing to me the way she did when I was a child. When my momma suggested to me that I seek God and ask for His help, that was God speaking through my momma.

God chose not to reprimand me that day and instead answered my prayer without hesitation. He restored my body and soul and asked only that I return to the main arena and treat my opponent as I would like my opponent to treat me. If I wanted to have dignity, I had to treat others with dignity. If I wanted to be treated with respect, I had to treat others with respect.

When I stepped into that arena and saw my opponent, I knew that I was a changed man. I had no desire to harm and humiliate him. I came to honor both of our God given talents. I didn't fight my opponent that day; I danced with him because, for the first time in my life, I saw another human being as a child of God. And I saw myself as a child of God. So I danced with my opponent that day—and I've been dancing with God's children ever since.

Coming home to the Father who made you is as natural as breathing air. And it's a homecoming without condemnation or reprimand or argument. It's a beautiful display of God's unconditional and undying love for His children.

The Solution to All Your Problems Is at Hand If Only You Will Ask

The greatest barrier to individual progress is a slavish devotion to precedent. If your life is filled with negative thoughts and actions that are undermining your happiness and your ability to enjoy life to the fullest, the solution is what the Bible refers to as a *renewal of the mind*, which I believe to be akin to a rebirth of one's spirit. "Be ye transformed by the renewal of the mind." Before I could begin walking in God's positive light, God had to first remove the cause of my negative thinking. Keep in mind that I said that God had to *remove the cause* of my negative thinking, not *change* my negative thinking.

I said earlier that we all have a cross to bear in life and that mine was that I was born into a world of oppression and racial prejudice. Throughout the many years that I was a full-blown racist, I always knew that the cause of my hatred of white people was rooted in the childhood years that I spent in the Deep South living under the Jim Crow laws. And I knew that this hatred carried over into my adolescent and adult years after my momma and I moved to California. And I understood what Maslow meant when he said, "There is no such thing as a well adjusted slave." You cannot get to a sense of purpose and live a life of harmony and balance while simultaneously allowing someone else to dictate your thoughts and actions. While I was able to recognize and have an intellectual understanding of *why* I became an anger-filled racist, I was unable to change *how* I felt inside.

The Bible says in 2 Corinthians 5:17, "Therefore, if anyone is in Christ, he is a new creation; old things have passed away; behold, all things have become new." The operative word in this verse is "new." It doesn't say "restore."

When I bought that 1954 Cadillac limousine in 1972, I *restored* it to its 1954 condition, but I didn't turn it into a *new* 1972 car. Prior to my kneeling in front of that toilet in Long Beach, I'd never before asked God into my life, so there was nothing for Him to restore. Instead, He made me new. The light of God in me was turned on for the first time. God didn't change a burned out light bulb. When I asked God to give me dignity, He did this by activating His love in me. It wasn't that His love wasn't in me, but that it wasn't active because I'd never asked God into my life. As a result, when I walked out to the main arena and looked at my opponent, I was incapable of hating him because I was looking at him with the love of God in my heart. While I was still aware of my oppressed childhood, the hate that it triggered in the past was gone. God had renewed my mind so that when I recalled my childhood in the Deep South, it didn't result in a knee-jerk reaction of anger. This renewal of my mind couldn't have been accomplished by the best psychiatrists in the world.

THE FEELING OF BEING SEPARATED

Around the time that I entered my teens, I sensed that my main problem in life was a feeling of separation, which in adulthood I more clearly defined as a separation from others, from God, and eventually from myself. While I couldn't define this feeling that clearly in my early childhood years, I surely felt it.

I firmly believe that all of us, to one degree or another, suffer from this terrible feeling of being disconnected. We didn't start out that way. Child psychologists have determined that newborn babies can't distinguish between themselves and their outer world. When a newborn lying in the crib looks up at a mobile, the baby actually thinks that the mobile is a part of itself.

It isn't long before newborns begin to feel that they are an entity unto themselves. Sigmund Freud defined one's ability to separate, or disconnect, oneself from others as the development of the human ego. The best definition I've heard of the human ego is "Edging God Out" because I believe that what we are disconnecting is the one thing we share in common, which is the God in each of us. The people who live in India are taught at an early age not to make this mistake. When they greet each other, they fold their hands and bow slightly, which is their way of acknowledging the God in others.

The Bible also says that "In Him we live and move and have our being" and "That which is made is not made of that which it doth appear. It's the evidence of, or the body of, the Creator." It is our belief in a separation from each other, and thus our separation from God, that keeps our goodness away from us.

Renowned American comparative psychologist Robert Yerkes, who conducted extensive work on the society of apes, reached the conclusion that "one chimpanzee is no chimpanzee." There is a similar Greek proverb "one man [is] no man." Put another way, Englishman John Donne pointed out that "no man is an island onto himself." What these learned men are saying is that we all need other people in order to feel human. God never meant for us to walk alone in life without Him or each other. We need each other in order to feel our human side just as much as we need God in order to feel our spiritual side.

We Are All Parts of the Whole

If our world populace is ever going to be able to live harmoniously, we have to find a way, as individuals as well as a collective world society, to acknowledge and respect the reality that we are all children of God. And it doesn't make any difference where someone lives, their nationality, their religious beliefs or lack thereof, their material worth, their level of education, or anything else. All that matters is that all of us are God's children. And the sooner we find a way to rejoice in knowing this, the sooner we're going to begin to live joyously together in a safe world.

When I served in Vietnam as a medic, I mentally divided soldiers who were brought to the White Elephant into two distinct and separate categories of black and white. If a white soldier was brought in, I referred to him as "the white guy in bed 26." If a black infantryman was brought in with a bullet wound in the leg, I referred to him as "the brother in bed 17."

Many of the soldiers who were treated at the White Elephant suffered from burns. One afternoon a soldier arrived on a stretcher, and from a distance it appeared to me that sections of his clothes had been separated from his body and were hanging over the sides of the stretcher, appearing like thin flaps.

As I arrived to help lift this severely burned soldier onto a gurney, at first glance I thought he was white. It wasn't until a few moments later that I realized he was a naked black man whose uniform had been removed prior to his being brought to the White Elephant. What I initially thought were thin flaps of his scorched dark uniform were actually large sections of his skin. I can still recall to this day looking down at that man and realizing that the difference between what I perceived as a black man and a white man boiled down to a layer of skin that was thinner than a sheet of cellophane I commonly used to wrap my sandwich.

Staring down at that soldier, I wondered if the color of this minute layer of skin was what those Jim Crow laws were fussing over. It would be another ten years before I recognized that my skin color had nothing to do with the problem white people had with me or the problem I had with them.

Robert Yerkes was right. Walking alone is not natural. One chimpanzee is no chimpanzee. God meant for us to enjoy the companionship of others—be they family, friends, loved ones, or even total strangers—regardless of race, age, gender, or their personal preferences.

I walked alone for 30 years, constantly separating myself from everyone and yet at the same time wanting so desperately to connect with them. Sartre was wrong. Hell is not other people. Heaven is other people because God resides in each of us. When I came to recognize this, my negative reactions toward others quickly began to dissipate.

Feeling Separated Isn't the Same as Being Different

While God never meant for us to feel separated from one another, He did intend to make us all uniquely different. How boring life would be if we were all physical clones of the same person who wanted all the same things in life. Wanting always to be smart, strong, successful, and right is like wanting always to have summer, daytime, sunshine, warmth, and 70 degrees. Not only is it impossible, it's boring. Although God meant for you to feel and be unique, He never meant for you to feel bad about it.

Never Allow Others to Negatively Define Your Uniqueness

The world without is merely a reflection of what you have acknowledged as true in your world within. The way you define yourself is based solely on what you accept and don't accept as being true.

The biggest mistake I made in my life was allowing others to place a negative connotation on my race. By affixing truth to those Jim Crow laws, I allowed others to define my being without ever questioning the validity of their reasons. As a result, until the age of 30, my insides didn't match my outsides.

In the Book of Proverbs, Solomon talks about how a man's words and actions can differ radically from what he feels in his heart. "As a man thinketh in his heart, so is he," clearly describes the painful dilemma that I faced for many years. It wasn't until God made me new by changing my heart that my negative self-image was transformed into a positive self-image.

The world in which you live is your world. The feelings you feel inside are your feelings. Accept the truths of others and your own truths only if they shine a positive light on your world and your personal being. God gave you the right to make these choices.

chapter fourteen

Prayers Answered

God has made it possible for you to realize your every dream by making it clear that you are capable of everything. Not just some things—but everything. "I can do all things through Christ who strengthens me." (Philippians 4:13).

For you to receive all the blessings that God has for you, you must reach a state of awe by accepting the fact that you are God's child, and that because God resides within you, there is nothing that you can't accomplish.

Not long ago, I counseled a couple who worried that they might not be able to afford a better home that they needed for their growing family.

The woman said to me, "Bishop, I just don't know if we'll be able to make that bigger mortgage payment."

I told her to forget about that house and start thinking about moving into an even more expensive house. The couple looked at me dumbfounded, as I continued, "If Jesus is to be believed, and He is, then according to His Word in John 14:12, you have the power within you to accomplish greater miracles than He did. If Jesus had the power to raise the dead and walk on water, surely God has given you the power to buy the house you want."

Jesus meant exactly what He said, and He understood the awesome capability and potential that God has bestowed upon you, and Jesus' message was—only believe.

There Are No Limits to God's Gifts

Never worry that what you're asking God to provide is too great. When you consider that God has the entire eternal universe at His disposal, God is fully capable of providing anything you might ask for.

Moreover, never worry that God may think that what you're asking for is beyond what you feel you're entitled to. Jesus said, "Do not fear, little flock, for it is your Father's good pleasure to give you the kingdom." (Luke 12:32). Note the wording "the kingdom." Jesus didn't say that God would be pleased to give you a *small morsel* from His kingdom or that God would give you *half* of the kingdom. The wording makes it clear that it pleases God to give His children *the entire* kingdom.

PRAYER AND MEDITATION

While I always believed there was a God, up until my championship fight in Long Beach, I didn't understand prayer because my momma always explained prayer by connecting it to faith and belief.

It is written, "Whatsoever you desire when you pray, believe that you have it and you'll receive it." As a child, this just didn't make any sense to me. How was I supposed to believe that I've got a bicycle that I don't have? What was I supposed to say to my friend Jeremy when I told him that I have a new bicycle at home, but if he wants to come over and ride it, I don't have it? I either believe I have that bicycle or I don't. And if I believe that I have it, then if I don't have it, I'm either delusional or I'm lying. I just couldn't make sense of it.

My problem was that I didn't understand that God has already agreed to give me anything I might pray for, providing that I believe His Word. Dr. Wayne Dyer said this more succinctly in the title of his book, *You'll See It When You Believe It*, which of course is the converse of the doubter's age-old words, "I'll believe it when I see it."

When Jesus spoke to Peter, He again connected God's answering our prayers to our limitless power of belief: "Have faith in God. Verily I say unto you, whosoever shall say unto this mountain, be thou taken up and cast into the sea; and shall not doubt in his heart, but shall believe that what he saith cometh to pass; he shall have it. Therefore I say unto you all things whatsoever ye pray for and ask for, believe that ye receive them, and ye shall have them."

For years I thought that God wasn't answering my momma's prayers because she lived from paycheck to paycheck. But I was wrong. Although I wasn't privy to what my momma prayed for in private, I know today that she never prayed for anything for herself. She prayed only for others. And the truth is that I know today, based on the intensity of my momma's faith, that had she asked God for a million dollars, God would have provided it.

To me, the irony would have been that had she received all that money on Monday, she would have given it all away by Friday. So God did provide for my momma's *every* need and answered her *every* prayer. My problem was that it took me the better part of 30 years to recognize that what my momma was praying for all her life wasn't what I thought she should be praying for.

God Sometimes Answers Prayer by Removing the Need

God doesn't always answer prayers by granting exactly what the person is praying for. A woman who is an obsessive spender might pray for more money in order to pay off her maxed-out credit cards. While God could increase the woman's finances, as an alternative He might elect to remove her need to shop. Both of God's answers would resolve the woman's problem. Removing her need to shop, however, would result in a better chance that her problem wouldn't return.

When I prayed to God prior to fighting for the World Championship, I asked Him to give me the strength to whup my opponent so that I might acquire dignity. God could have given me the strength and wherewithal to give my opponent a sound and humiliating whupping. Instead, God removed my desire to beat up my opponent. By changing my heart, God enabled me to acquire the dignity I was praying for by treating my opponent with respect.

Before praying to God, think about exactly what it is that you want. If you're unmarried and pray to God to provide you with a spouse, are you asking God for a spouse because you have a great deal of love that you want to share with another person, or are you asking God for a spouse because you're lonely? If the latter better defines your motivation, it might be better to share with God that you're lonely and ask Him to decide how best to resolve this.

Oftentimes the thought of God removing our need rather than granting our prayer can be unsettling. A person who is overweight might be uncomfortable with the notion of God removing their desire for sweets because sweets are a comforter, just as the person who strives to be a millionaire may, out of fear of being poor, become uneasy over the idea of God removing the need for money. If you find yourself faced with this dilemma, don't worry. God is a loving God, who knows your needs before you ask. My personal experience and belief is that God never closes a door without opening another.

Don't Expect God to Grant a Prayer that He Knows Will Be Misused

After years of studying and teaching the martial arts, I found that there are, generally speaking, two main types of people who want to learn karate—one, those who honestly feel that they can't defend themselves and want to learn self defense to become secure in their surroundings and, two, bullies who want to become better bullies.

Over time, I've come to view money in much the same way. People who pursue money are motivated either by a desire to use money to better their lives and the lives of others, or they're obsessed with using money to control their environment and flaunt their wealth.

I believe that God knew that had I acquired wealth prior to winning the World Championship in 1977, I would have used money to make others miserable. Prior to 1977, there was no question in my mind that I had every intention of using wealth in order to raise myself above white people so that I could look down at them and treat them as badly as they'd treated me. And if I knew this, God surely knew it.

"In the Name of Jesus" Isn't a Rubber Stamp

Occasionally, people have said to me, "Bishop, the Bible says that if I ask God for something in the name of Jesus that my prayer will be answered. For years I've ended every prayer by telling God that I'm asking in the name of Jesus, but a lot of my prayers were never answered."

These people, of course, are referring to John 14:12-14, which says, "And whatsoever you shall ask in My name, that I will do, that the Father may be glorified in the Son. If you ask anything in My name, I will do it."

The difficulty that these people have is that they don't recognize that the *name* and the *spirit* of Jesus are one. "Whatsoever you shall ask in My name" means that you pray with the intensity that Jesus prayed, as well as have the intensity of his faith.

Praying to God in the spirit that Jesus prayed also means that what you're asking God for in prayer will glorify the Father.

When we truly love God, all the things that we receive from prayer become a means of glorifying Him. When we're filled with peace and joy, it is because we know we have His blessings on us.

Jesus meant that He would do whatever you ask in His name. All that you need do is love and trust Him, and then ask in His name. Jesus wants you to ask; He expects you to ask; He waits eagerly to perform greater works in and through your life.

THE PROPER PERSPECTIVE ON
MATERIAL THINGS AND MONETARY WEALTH

Beginning at around the age of ten, I became obsessed with becoming rich, and I used to tell my brother Marion that one day I would drive an expensive car and live in a mansion.

Wanting to become rich and famous was more than a childhood dream. Becoming a millionaire was going to change people's perception of me. Acquiring riches was my way of getting out of that weather-beaten shack on stilts and those ugly pair of shoes and ill-fitting hand-me-downs. If there was one Bible verse that would have jumped out at me, it would have been Ecclesiastes 10:19 that says, "But money answers everything."

Today I understand that the reference is to money on earth, not in heaven, and that one shouldn't love money or become obsessed with obtaining it. But no one could have convinced me of that when I lived in Savannah, Georgia.

Being poor became strongly enmeshed with my self image. When I saw on television that 300-pound black woman playing the role of a maid, I thought she was truly successful. And I felt bad when I compared that maid to my momma, who worked as a maid for lower middleclass families. In my mind, the two maids didn't match. The one on television lived in the nicely furnished maid's quarters of a mansion, while my momma walked home alone through those dark woods to a shack where she shared a bed with three kids. To me, successful maids worked in the mansions of white people. It never once entered my mind that the black maid I saw on TV—or any black person in Georgia, for that matter—could ever *own* a mansion.

Scarcity Thinking

Many people who believe that they live empty of necessities because they're either unlucky or unfortunate or both, fail to recognize that God wants His children to enjoy all the comforts of life and is eager to supply us these things in great abundance.

I think it's unfortunate that today many black churchgoers still aren't being taught about success, but instead continue to believe what my mother was taught years ago, that poverty is a good thing. I believe that people need to learn that monetary success is meaningful to being a Christian because it's important that they pay their bills and provide their kids with a decent education—and they can't do this if they're broke.

When Jesus gave His Sermon on the Mount, He encouraged His followers not to worry about their worldly needs. Elsewhere in the Bible, human needs are again mentioned, "Do not worry about your life, what you will eat or what you will drink; nor about your body, what you will put on." (Matthew 6:25).

Jesus didn't chastise His followers for having needs, but validated their needs as a part of being human. At another time, Christ told His followers that the way to having their needs fulfilled was through prayer—"Ask and it shall be given"—and all that was required of them was that they believe.

If you have even the slightest reservation about God's intention, take a look at Nature's abundance. Do you honestly believe that He meant for you to have less? God's blessings are piled high for you. All that is necessary is for you to have the faith to "prove me herewith."

The Proper Use of Money and Notoriety

In Luke 16: 1-13, Jesus makes an interesting comment about stewardship in general. He says, "He who is faithful in what is least is faithful also in much; and he who is unjust in what is least is unjust also in much." In other words, the person who begins with very little and becomes successful—the age-old rags-to-riches story—will become even more successful when that person is given much more.

Today I view money as a means through which I can help others rather than an end in itself. Before I became a pastor, my intention was to have money come to me and end with me because I felt that the only purpose of money was to prove to others that I was a success. When I was a young man, I didn't know anyone who was both successful and didn't have money. Today I know a good number of people who aren't wealthy but who lead highly successful lives.

The Bible teaches us not to pursue money, not to love money, and not to allow money to become one's god. On the other hand, the Bible also makes numerous references to tithing and acts of charity by instructing us to "Give and it shall be given back to you." Surely God is aware that we can't give what we don't have. Be comforted by the assurance that God will continue to bless you as long as you keep your high level of faith and use money to help do His work.

On a personal level, I'm motivated to succeed monetarily because to be viewed as a man who lives comfortably shows people what God not only *can* do, but *will* do. To those people whose lives are negatively impacted by impoverished thinking, my material rewards are visual proof of my faith in God, as well as my desire to glorify Him.

Clarify Your Motivation

If you presently find yourself driven by a strong desire for money that you don't have, spend a half hour and do the following. Take a blank piece of paper and draw a line down the center, and then draw a big plus sign at the top of the left side and a big minus sign at the top of the right side.

Now relax for a minute, and then imagine that you've just won $10,000,000 in the lottery. Allow your mind to wander, and in your imagination start spending that money. When your thoughts are in order, write down what you purchased, listing the item in either the plus or minus column. This will take a fair degree of honesty. If you purchased a new house and can honestly admit that you did so in order to make your brother's home seem like a room at the Motel Six, then enter it in the minus column. If you purchased that home so that your kids will have their own bedrooms and your wife will have a better kitchen, write your house purchase into the plus column. Continue spending your money and listing your purchases in the appropriate columns, and when you've finished, add up the pluses and minuses.

If you find that the number of minuses is greater than the number of pluses, you know the reason why God hasn't answered your prayers. On the other hand, if you find the reverse to be true, then either you're not praying correctly and/or your faith in God needs to be strengthened.

Viewed in a positive light, remember that God always knows what's best for you. Be assured that if your motivation isn't right or your faith is weak, He will readily answer your prayer for improved finances as soon as you take the necessary steps to change your motivation and/or strengthen your faith.

LIVING IN GOD ISN'T A FREE RIDE

Having entered into a living partnership with God, I'm no longer a racist. Before I allowed God into my heart, I hated white people and a whole lot more about the world in which I lived. For 30 years, although I *knew* a lot about God, I continued to feel separated from everything and everybody because I didn't *do* anything. I learned from experience that you can live yourself into right thinking, but you can't think yourself into right living. It's far easier to have a religious philosophy than to live one.

Faith Without Works Is Dead

On the day that I prayed in front of that toilet, I finally accepted the truth of my momma's words and believed (1) that God exists, (2) that I'd acquired a strong faith and belief in Him, and (3) that God was capable of answering all of my prayers. Then a short while after God renewed my body and mind and I won the championship, I soon forgot about my promise to serve Him.

The problem was that winning the World Championship resulted in a degree of overnight notoriety, and I returned to my old ways of seeking fame and fortune. Because I had free will, God allowed me to wrongly use the dignity that He gave me on the day I won the championship for my own selfish needs.

Five years passed before I learned the biblical wisdom of "Faith without works is dead."

The faith is faith in God, not in things of the world; and the works specifically refers to God's work. Not keeping my promise to God truly did result in my "dying faith." Becoming willing to leave my old path and return to walking with God is what eventually led to my building The Family Church International—and I've been on that path ever since.

chapter fifteen

Keys to Staying Connected

The fundamental story of my life is the same as the story of your life. At birth, we felt intimately connected to others, to God, and to ourselves. We were an integral part of the whole, and the world in which we lived was a loving and secure place because we were still home with God.

Then the time arrived when we left our Father's house, and the feeling of being separated from the whole set in and grew worse through the years. Up until the time we allow God back into our lives, all the problems we create and face are the direct result of our desperate battle to return to the Father.

What follows represents ways of living and thinking that, when faithfully adhered to on a daily basis, help assure that we will never leave home again.

"There is time enough for everything." –Jiddu Krishnamurti

I recently heard about a couple who were married for 72 years and lived in the same house where they raised four children. Victor and Elizabeth lived in New Jersey in a three-story home that included a large basement.

Victor was a quiet man whose many years of living had resulted in considerable wisdom. One evening after dinner, he was asked how he'd managed to stay married to the same woman for all those years while living in the same house. After pausing in thought for several moments, he drew on his pipe and then replied, "Patience."

All the major religions speak of patience being the great virtue, and the Bible relates patience to faith: ". . . the testing of your faith produces patience." (James 1:2). There is no need to be in such a big hurry to get everything done so that life will be exactly the way you want it. Instead of chasing life, do as Victor did and let life come to you.

Live Each Day As If It Were Your Last

Many of us have heard the saying "Live today as if it were the first day of your life." Personally, I think our lives would be more in line with the basic principles of God's Word if we lived each day as if it were our last because doing so would result in a major shift in our priorities.

If you knew this was your last day on earth, you would no longer have the option of putting off resolving a problem today because you think you could address it tomorrow or next week or next year, which unfortunately often turns out to be too late.

Do yourself a great service and tomorrow morning when you awaken, spend 30 minutes quietly by yourself and write down how you would live out this particular day if you knew it were your last. I guarantee that if you were completely honest with yourself, the schedule that you would write down for the last day of your life would be nothing like the schedule you would have written if this same day were the first day of your life.

Now cross out everything on your list that would bring gratification to *you alone*. If you wrote down that you would spend the day at Disneyland or would have bought that new piece of wardrobe you've longed to wear or that car you've always wanted to drive—even if only for one day—cross those off your list.

Now draw a big circle around the activities that you know would bring peace of mind to *others*. For example, calling your children or parents to tell them how much you love them and how important they've been in your life or patching up an argument with a close friend whom you haven't spoken with in two years or fixing the strained relations with your neighbor by apologizing for the harsh words you spoke a year ago after your neighbor complained about your son's loud music—draw a big circle around all such entries on your "last day" schedule. These are things that you made a top priority because you knew there would be no tomorrow.

Finally, recognize that you've remained hesitant about taking action on the items on your list because you felt you would have many tomorrows. Then simply ask God to give you the strength and guidance you need in order to act on the items on your list. If you'll follow what I've suggested, you'll be both amazed and pleased by the results—as will those you love and value.

Align Your Motivation with God's Love

When I was competing on the karate tournament circuit, making my opponents look bad was as important to me as making myself look good. I'd taunt and ridicule my opponents before the match, during the match, and after the match. At the end of the day, all I had accomplished was to widen the gap of separation between myself and others.

I recently heard about a college track coach who often told his runners, "If you can't win the race, make the guy in front of you break the record." I think that's beautiful and in accordance with the way God wants His children to treat one another when competing.

Unfortunately, our society is becoming increasingly focused on winning. From the kid playing high school football to the highest corporate executive, the main objective is to win no matter what the cost and no matter who gets hurt. The old saying "Keeping up with the Joneses" has become "Beating down the Joneses."

If you want to make your life more comfortable and enjoyable, embrace the idea that the only person you're competing with is yourself. Your own personal betterment is all that really matters. And when you do find yourself in competition with an opponent— be it on the playing field or in business or anywhere else—dance with the opponent. As Colonel Slade said in the film *Scent of a Woman*, "If you get tangled up, tango on."

Envision a scenario where you're on a football team and playing the position of a pass defender. The ball is hiked, and the opposing team's wide receiver takes off for the end zone. You pick him up around mid-field and run alongside him all the way to the end zone where he makes a spectacular leaping catch for a touchdown.

Imagine saying to your opponent who just scored the touchdown, "Unbelievable, Mike—what a great catch! I thought I had that pass blocked, but when I saw that I didn't, I was with you all the way. I'm sure the fans enjoyed it. And thanks for showing me an area of my game that I need to work on. I appreciate it."

Remember that in all areas of your life where you're in competition with others, whenever you make your competitor look and feel good, you make yourself look and feel good. What you sow, you reap.

Acceptance versus Understanding

There's been a great movement over the past several decades for people to learn to accept the lifestyles, behaviors, thoughts, and actions of others. "Live and let live" has become a poster slogan for acceptance. When I was a racist, people would say to me, "Donnie, just accept the fact that there are a good many white people walking around who simply have it out for black folks." These individuals thought the way for me to get rid of my anger was to accept their right to live their lives the way they chose and to have their own opinions.

They were telling me that my anger was being caused by my unwillingness to accept prejudice. I couldn't accept prejudice then, and I don't accept it now because I believe that there are things in life that God doesn't expect us to accept. Surely God doesn't expect any of us to accept alcohol and drug addiction in others, any more than He expects parents to accept their underage child having sex.

When you find it impossible to accept things or situations in life, rather than battling with acceptance, strive for *understanding*. As a preacher, I can't and don't accept homosexuality because it goes against the Word of God. I know there are people who disagree with this position, but this is my belief based on my study of the Bible. Today, while I still don't accept homosexuality, I've taken the time to understand homosexuality and the need some people have to live a homosexual lifestyle.

Do Not Judge

For many years I walked around judging others because I felt that my judgments defined them. The truth is that our judgments define ourselves by defining our likes and dislikes.

There's an old adage in psychology that says, "You know, there's something about that old boy that I can't stand about me." Much of my displeasure with others was my way of avoiding something inside me. I didn't like rich people because I was poor. I didn't like educated people because I felt that I wasn't educated. I didn't like going to church because I felt that all the people who were there understood God while I didn't.

Judging the lives of others only made me miserable because my judgments of others didn't result in their changing anything about themselves. The fact that I disliked white people and reacted with hostility toward them didn't change the manner in which many whites treated me, and in fact often caused some to treat me worse.

Our relationships with others are based on liking and disliking. And when we feel separated from others, we look for the things we don't like about them. Our judgments are designed to make the statement that our way is better and that we are superior. Unfortunately, this attitude serves only to increase our separation and, hence, our suffering.

Trust Truth and Honesty

When it comes to living life with ourselves and others, as well as communicating with ourselves, God, and others, there is no greater power than the truth.

The first time in my life that I shared the complete honest truth about my life with another human being was the night that I talked with Valerie. My willingness to do this came on the heels of my giving up trying to gain her affection by playing a role that wasn't a true representation of who I really was.

Thankfully, Valerie had enough patience and cared enough about me and about us to hold her ground. While I was trying to lure her into the bedroom, she was focusing on becoming my friend. It's been wisely said that a true friend is someone who reaches out for your hand and touches your heart. Through her friendship, Valerie indeed touched my heart.

One of the most clever and profound definitions I've heard of intimacy is "in-to-me-you-see." Before I met Valerie, I didn't think that any woman would be interested in me if I told her the truth about my childhood growing up in poverty in the Deep South, that my father had abandoned me at birth, and that my racist attitude had more to do with my shortcomings than it did with white people. But there was something different about Valerie that caused me to feel safe with her. The only other person I felt that way about was my momma. And so late one night I got honest—pulled out all the stops and just told her the pure unadulterated truth about myself and let the chips fall where they may.

The Bible says, "And you shall know the truth, and the truth shall make you free." The truth of those words was made clear on the night I shared the truth of my life with Valerie. As things turned out, when I was finished, she was far more attracted to the real Donnie Williams than she was to the hip, slick, and cool Donnie Williams who thought he could get whatever he wanted by playing the role of "the man."

Eventually over time, Valerie forced me to see myself differently. She was the first woman besides my momma who said to me, "You've got it." I owe a great debt to Valerie, who over time helped build my self confidence to the point that I wasn't angry anymore.

God often speaks to us through people, which I believe was what occurred on the night that Valerie, after hearing the truth of my life story, gave me a new and positive perspective of myself. She wouldn't have succeeded in getting far, however, had I not been willing to listen. Learning how to listen is another gift that Valerie taught me. Prior to her, I rarely listened to anyone. I'd look right at them and give the impression that I was listening, but I wasn't hearing anything they were saying.

Today I often encounter this when counseling kids who are having problems at home, in school, in the street, and particularly with drugs. I recently talked with a teenager who'd just gotten out of rehab and relapsed. He'd been rushed to the emergency room on more than one occasion, and I was convinced that if he didn't change his ways, he'd either wind up dead or in juvenile hall.

After talking for a half hour, I realized that this kid wasn't listening and heatedly said, "Why aren't you listening to me? I'm trying to save your life, for God's sake, why can't you listen to me?" But he chose not to hear me because he didn't see things the way I did.

I've encountered the same communication breakdown with married couples and individuals who are having a difficult time connecting with God. The problem is that these people either don't have the ability or the desire to listen to someone who is sincerely and honestly trying to help them.

The Bible says in John 8:43, "Why do you not understand my speech? Because you are not able to listen to My word." If you or someone you know has difficulty listening, as I did for most of my life, consider that while you recognize the voice of the person speaking to you, the message being conveyed may well be from God and may also be the answer to the problem being discussed.

God Wants You to Grow

There is wisdom in the words of Neale Donald Walsh who said, "Life begins outside your comfort zone." Throughout your lifetime, God wants you to continue to grow on all levels, and in order for you to do this, you must be willing to push yourself.

God gave you intelligence because He wants you to learn. He gave you a physical body, which He expects you to keep healthy and continue to strengthen. He gave you emotions so that you can enjoy your life to the fullest, and He gave you a spirit so that you can always be close to Him.

God wants you to go beyond your self-imposed limits. If you think that graduating high school is the best you can do, enroll in junior college. If you've always felt that you have two left feet on the dance floor, take up ballroom dancing and plan on winning contests. If fear of being rejected has caused you not to date, invite the person you've been attracted to for six months to join you for dinner. And if you feel that your spirit is in limbo, strengthen your faith and belief in God and watch the boundaries of your self-imposed limits begin to widen.

Be Careful What Seeds You Plant

The Bible says that we reap what we sow, which certainly proved to be true in my life. After spending years being a racist, when I finally found the woman of my dreams in Valerie, because of the color of my skin, her father rejected me and disowned her.

You can't plant lettuce in the spring and then three months later walk out into your lettuce fields expecting to find avocado trees. You're going to find lettuce.

For many years of my life I planted seeds of hate, blame, judgment, and revenge while at the same time anticipating that people would reward my efforts with respect and dignity. Instead, what I got back was a whole lot of negativity, so much so that I ended up in front of that toilet praying to God to throw me a desperately-needed lifeline.

God gave you the free will to choose the seeds you plant in your garden. He gave you the land, rich soil, plenty of water, a wide array of seeds, and then appointed you as gardener. The choice is yours to plant a beautiful garden or a weed patch.

Practice Compassion

Webster's dictionary defines compassion as "Sympathetic consciousness of others' distress together with a desire to alleviate it." Doesn't the above definition describe the life of Jesus? Wasn't the primary goal of His life's work and His teaching to alleviate the distress of others? And has there ever in the history of mankind been a greater example of a person showing compassion for others than when Jesus died on the Cross for the sins of the world?

If the Word of God instructs us to model our actions and thoughts after Jesus, then it behooves us to be compassionate toward others. Today when I find myself at odds with another person, I look beyond the individual and see the God within.

An old and wise film director friend of mine once said that life is built on second chances, and if it isn't, none of us has a career. I would take that one step further and say that life is built on an infinite number of chances if for no other reason than Jesus has already paid for all of our sins, not just two of them. If giving me a lifetime of chances to make good is good enough for Jesus, then my giving everyone else a lifetime of chances is good enough for me.

Hatred Breeds Blame

Blame is the apron-tugging offspring of hatred. When I became obsessed with becoming rich and famous and using money and power to control others, I presented myself with a great opportunity to practice blame as a way of life. Blaming others for all my problems was my way of justifying my hostile behavior and unkind words.

Failure to succeed in life through hatred taught me a valuable lesson. While the effect my hatred had on white people was negligible, the effect this same hatred had on me was monumental. There are good reasons for this.

Living my life based on blaming white people was self-destructive. By blaming white people, I essentially made sure that the Jim Crow laws accomplished what they were intended to do—to make me feel oppressed. If I didn't feel oppressed, then I wouldn't be blaming white people or the Jim Crow laws.

As long as I blamed others for my low self-esteem and lack of dignity, I had to wait for them to change before I could feel better, but when God renewed my mind, it became unnecessary for me to blame anyone else for any of my problems. As a result, those Jim Crow laws were disempowered and no longer had a negative effect on me.

Practice Forgiveness

Mark Twain once wrote, "Forgiveness is the fragrance the violet sheds on the heel that has crushed it." I think that's a beautiful description of forgiveness.

It was extremely hard for me to forgive the people who had directly and indirectly been the cause of my becoming filled with hate. But I knew that I had to. Why? Because I'd learned that if I didn't forgive these people, I'd have to keep blaming them. And I knew that blame begets judgment begets anger begets hatred. And I'd already had more than my share of those things in my life, so I had to forgive those who had wronged me.

More important, I believe that what's written in the Bible is the complete Word of God. Not *some* of what is written is *some* of God's Word, but *all* of what is written is *all* of God's Word. And so I either believe all of what's contained in the Bible, or I believe none of it. I can't just choose what chapters and verses work for me and toss out what doesn't.

In Matthew 5:44, Jesus says, "But I say to you, love your enemies, bless those who curse you, do good to those who hate you, and pray for those who spitefully use you and persecute you." According to the words that came directly from the mouth of Jesus, I'm supposed to love, bless, do good things for, and pray for white people—and I can't do any of those things unless I first forgive them.

Jesus, Himself, set an example on the day that He was crucified. If Jesus could ask God to forgive the soldiers who were in the process of killing Him, shame on me if I can't find it in my heart to forgive those who have caused me to feel bad about the color of my skin.

Living Life Based on Revenge

By the mid-1970s my hip, slick, and cool black power gig was in full swing. I was being driven around in my limousine and storming into karate tournaments, flaunting my capes and floppy hats and marching alongside my badass BKF comrades in arms.

Then the day arrived in August 1977 when a white man publicly insulted and vilified me in front of the marital arts community. He told me a lot of things that I didn't want to hear, and I became enraged.

The message I heard from him was that I was worse than a wannabe—I was a never-was. If none of what the man said was true, his words wouldn't have bothered me. The problem was that while many people who were present didn't believe him, I believed him. Deep inside, regardless of how I appeared to others, the words that man shouted in my face hit a deep nerve.

There's an old Chinese proverb that says, "One who pursues revenge should dig two graves." This was surely true in my young adulthood. I was angry that white people had disrespected my people and treated us as inferior. My anger eventually turned to hatred. I awoke to it in the morning and went to bed with it at night. I carried it on my shoulders and often vented it with my words and actions.

It was bad enough that the oppression and prejudice of the Deep South resulted in my feeling isolated and inferior when I lived in Georgia. For me to seek revenge by becoming a racist when I moved to California allowed the Jim Crow laws to continue to control my inner and outer life well into my adulthood.

The irony was that while I was going around spewing my hatred at the world, the white people whom I blamed for causing my fierce racism continued to go about their business without a care in the world as to how Donnie Williams was doing, let alone feeling.

PARTING THOUGHTS

With God in My Life I Am Never Alone

I don't believe there is a worse negative emotion than the feeling of loneliness. *Being* alone isn't the same as *feeling* lonely. I can attend a professional football game and be in a crowd of 75,000 complete strangers and, although sitting alone by myself, not feel lonely.

It is the God within me that continually connects with the God within others that gives me a feeling of being part of the human race rather than being separated from it. Today I have a special and highly personal relationship with the God who made me, and wherever I am, He is.

Doing God's Will

Every morning I pray to God to tell me His will for me and to give me the strength to carry it out. I do this not only because I promised God that I would serve Him, but because I've learned that structuring my life around God's will, instead of my own will, results in God blessing my life as well as the lives of those I touch.

I no longer harbor any animosity toward white people or any other race of people because I now know who they are—they're God's children, and in so being, we're all family because we share the same Father. Because I believe that God's will for me is to serve Him by being of service to His children, I named my church The Family Church.

Living to Glorify God

For many years of my life, the purpose and goal of everything I did was to glorify myself. When I won a karate tournament, I took all the glory. Whenever I appeared in a movie, I pointed at my name in the credits and took all the credit. In everything I did, I was the creator and the unmoved mover, and I made sure that everyone knew that all the glory belonged to me.

Today my only desire is to glorify God because I know that by myself I can do nothing. The Bible says that "It is the Father within me that doeth the works" and "All things are from God." God built The Family Church through me. Although I did much of God's work, without Him, the church would still be an auto repair shop. The beauty of working for God instead of myself is that it makes it unnecessary for me to spend another minute trying to convince anyone of how great I am, and what a tremendous load off my shoulders this has been.

I want to thank you for allowing me the opportunity to share with you my life and the lessons I've learned. It's my sincere hope that this book has helped to enrich your life. If I can be of service to you in any way, please feel free to contact me through www.thefamilychurch.com.

About the Contributors

Tom Bleecker began his writing career in 1970 under the mentorship of Oscar-winning screenwriter and director Blake Edwards. After writing for screen and television for nearly 30 years, Bleecker coauthored his first book with Linda Lee, *The Bruce Lee Story* (Ohara Publications, 1988). Several books followed, including Bleecker's second book on Lee, *Unsettled Matters*, which became a bestseller, *The Journey* (Gilderoy Publications, 2001), and *Inside U: How to Become the Master of Your Own Destiny* by Grandmaster Byong Yu, Ph.D., with Tom Bleecker (Hay House, 2003). Bleecker's most current film "The Jacket" was released through Warner Brothers in March 2005.

Joe Hyams reported from Hollywood for the *New York Herald Tribune* from 1951 to 1964 and, in addition to the martial arts classic *Zen in the Martial Arts*, is the author of 37 books, including biographies on Humphrey Bogart, former President George Bush, and actor/icon James Dean. The author lives in Penrose, Colorado with his wife Lisa.